Blacks Tourist's Guide To Scotland

Adam Black

BLACK'S TOURIST'S GUIDE

TO

SCOTLAND

FOURTH EDITION

EDINBURGH
ADAM AND CHARLES BLACK
1881

THE FALL OF FOYERS: INVERNESS-SHIRE.

CONTENTS.

4
1

3
5

8

0
2

'THE LAND OF MOUNTAIN AND OF FLOOD,'

is distinguished for the beauty and variety of its scenery. These features it acquires from its rugged mountains, its clear and swiftly-flowing rivers, and its lochs and firths. The latter so penetrate the whole coast, that there is actually no place inland more than 40 miles from the sea. The country is divided naturally into *Highlands and Lowlands*, although there is no exact line of demarcation between the two; and for civil purposes into counties and parishes. About a century and a half ago, the state of Scotland, especially the Highland portion, somewhat resembled that of England previous to the Norman Conquest. The inhabitants were divided into tribes called *Clans*, each of which had its particular chief, whose consequence and security depended on the number of his retainers. The rents of these vassals were paid chiefly in military service, so that a proprietor's wealth was estimated not so much by the produce of his land as by the number of men he could bring into the field. These clans were at constant feud with each other, and their independent spirit kept the country in a state of constant agitation and insecurity. This state of society was completely changed at the time of *the Union* of Scotland with

England, when the clans of the Borders were dissolved, and the power of the Highland clans brought into subjection, although several of them remain nominally to the present time.

Scotland is famed for its mountains and lakes. The mountains consist both of detached groups and chains. Of the latter the most celebrated are the Grampians, extending from the south-eastern boundaries of Argyleshire to the heart of Aberdeenshire. This chain may be regarded as a natural rampart, forming the south-eastern boundary of the Highlands.

Moors and Deer-forests.—Scotland contains extensive tracts of land composed of morasses, intermixed with rocks, lakes, and peat-moss. The principal of these are situated in the counties of Perth, Aberdeen, Inverness, Ross, and Sutherland. They afford excellent grouse-shooting, and are also used for pasture. The deer-forests differ from the moors in being wholly given over to sport.

The Rivers of Scotland are generally rapid, and diversified by rocks and cataracts. Except the Clyde, few of them are navigable to any great extent. The *Tweed* rises near the sources of the Annan and Clyde, and running past Peebles through a beautiful pastoral country, falls into the German Ocean at Berwick-upon-Tweed, after a winding course of about 100 miles. The *Forth* rises on the east of Ben Lomond, and receiving the waters of the Teith and the Allan, it becomes a considerable stream at Stirling, to which the tide flows, and to which it is navigable for small vessels. The *Tay* rises to the north of Loch Lomond ; and, expanding into the romantic sheet of water called Loch Tay, flows in a circuitous route past Dunkeld and Perth, and falls into the Firth of Tay at the confluence of its waters with the Earn, about twenty miles from the mouth of the estuary. It is navigable to Perth. It is the largest of Scottish, and, in respect to the volume of water it conveys to the sea, even of British rivers. The *North* and *South Esk* have their source in the Grampians, and fall into the sea at Montrose within three miles of each other. The *Dee* and the *Don* have also their rise in the Grampians, and fall into the sea at Aberdeen.

Lochs.—Of the fresh-water lochs or lakes in Scotland the most celebrated, as well as the largest, is Loch Lomond, a noble sheet of water about 24 miles in length ; its greatest breadth being 10 miles. Loch Katrine in Perthshire is one of the most romantic. Besides these the others most worthy of notice are Lochs Tay, Awe, Tummel, Rannoch, and Earn, situated in Perthshire and Argyleshire ; the Caledonian Canal lochs and Loch Laggan in Inverness-shire ; Loch Maree in Ross-shire, and Shin in Sutherlandshire.

Agriculture.—Both the law and the practice of Scotland are favourable to agricultural enterprise. What in England are termed "tenants at will," or tenants without a lease, are unknown in Scotland. Leases may be said to be universal, extending to fifteen, nineteen, or twenty-one years. It was not uncommon, indeed, about fifty years ago, and before that time, to give liferents, or leases for twice nineteen years or even longer, a circumstance highly favourable to enterprise on the part of the tenant. With the exception of some districts in the Highlands and Islands, the system of small farms has been abandoned, and has given way to farms of great extent, rented by persons of intelligence and capital. There are no tithes.

Law Courts.—The supreme *Civil* court of Scotland is called the Court of Session. It holds two sessions annually, in the Parliament House, Edinburgh. The number of judges is thirteen. They are styled Lords of Session, and sit in two sets of courts or chambers, called the *Outer* and *Inner* Houses. The judges who sit in the outer house are called Lords Ordinary, and there is appeal from their decisions to the Inner House. The Inner House is divided into First and Second Divisions, which form, in effect, two courts of equal and independent authority. The supreme *Criminal* court (called the High Court of Justiciary) consists of six judges, who are also judges of the Court of Session. The President of the whole Court is the *Lord Justice-General*, and the President of the Second Division is called the *Lord Justice-Clerk*. In the spring and autumn vacations the judges hold circuits in the chief provincial towns, two going each circuit. The inferior courts of law include those of the Sheriff, police, and justices of the peace.

The Kirk.—Every parish in Scotland enjoys the privilege of having a resident clergyman and schoolmaster, the number of parishes being 918, and clergy about 1400. The national form of church government is the Presbyterian. It was established in 1690 by Act of Parliament, and afterwards secured by the Treaty of Union. The adherents of Presbyterianism are further comprised in the United Presbyterian and Free Churches, which are offshoots from the parent church, and thus hold almost identical opinions. The church government is vested in kirk-sessions, presbyteries, synods, and the General Assembly. The Scottish Episcopal Church consists of seven Dioceses, with a corresponding number of bishops, one of whom is elected Primus. The Roman Catholic Church is divided into three districts—east, west, and north, and has an archbishop and two bishops.

Universities.—There are four Universities in Scotland, which, in order of their foundations, are as follow :—St. Andrews, 1413 ; Glasgow, 1450 ; Aberdeen, 1494 ; and Edinburgh, 1582. There are two Episcopal Colleges—one at Glenalmond, Perthshire, and another at Millport, Buteshire. The University of St. Andrews consisted at one time of three colleges, viz. St. Salvador's, St. Leonard's, and St. Mary's ; but in 1748, the first two were united, and the buildings of St. Leonard's were alienated and converted into dwelling-houses. The University of Aberdeen consists of two united colleges—King's, founded as above stated ; and Marischal, instituted and endowed by George Keith, Earl Marischal, in 1593. From an early period Scotland enjoyed special educational advantages. By an Act passed in the reign of William and Mary it was enacted that there should be a school and schoolmaster in every parish. This provision has been continued by the establishment of public schools under school-boards. Besides these, there are numerous endowed schools connected with the various religious sects. The children attending these schools are taught the ordinary branches, and pay a very small fee.

Parliamentary Representation.—There are 88 Peers of Scotland, who, by the Treaty of Union, elect 16 of their number as their representatives in the House of Lords for a single Parliament. The number of members of Parliament is 60.

Commerce and Manufactures.—The principal seaports in Scotland are Glasgow, Greenock, Leith, Dundee, and Aberdeen. The exports consist of cotton and linen stuffs, yarn and wool, silk goods, iron, coal, spirits and beer, black cattle, herrings, salmon, etc. The principal imports are grain, tea, sugar, coffee, tobacco, wine, raw cotton, flax, hemp, raw silk, dye stuffs, etc. The *Linen Manufacture* was the earliest, and long regarded as the staple, branch of industry carried on in Scotland. Dundee, and the east of Scotland, including Fifeshire, are the great seats of this manufacture, particularly in sheetings, Osnaburgs, sail-cloth, and the coarser fabrics ; and Dunfermline, with the neighbouring towns and villages, the principal seat of damask, diaper, and the finer fabrics. Lanarkshire and the contiguous counties of Renfrew and Ayr are the principal seats of the *iron and cotton manufacture.* Some of the cotton fabrics made at Glasgow and Paisley are of almost unrivalled beauty and fineness. The *woollen and worsted factories* are situated chiefly at Aberdeen, Hawick, Galashiels, and Jedburgh, and in the counties of Stirling, Clackmannan, Argyle, and Inverness. Hawick is celebrated for its manufacture of woollen hose, blankets, and flannels ; Stirling and Bannockburn for tartans ; Kilmarnock for carpets, shawls, and nightcaps. *Ship-building* is carried on to a great extent on the banks of the Clyde near Glasgow, Dumbarton, and Greenock ; as also at Leith, the neighbourhood of Kirkcaldy (Fife), Dundee, and Aberdeen. *Brewing* and *Distilling* are branches of trade to which Scotland has been long addicted. The fisheries are abundant.

Banking in Scotland is carried on by means of joint-stock companies ; and, except in the case of chartered banks, each partner is responsible to the extent of his private fortune. Sums are received as low as £10 as deposits, and interest is allowed at a little below the market rate. The system of " cash accounts " is peculiar to the Scotch banks, and consists of a credit given to an individual with two or more collateral securities. The Act prohibiting the circulation of small notes in England did not extend to Scotland ; so that the currency consists almost ex-clusively of paper notes of £1 and upwards.

The Population of Scotland, according to the Census of 1871. was 3,358,613, and its increase at decennial periods since

1,608,420 ; (1811) 1,805,864 ; (1821) 2,091,521 ; (1831) 2,364,386 ; (1841) 2,620,184 ; (1851) 2,888,742 ; (1861) 3,062,294 ; (1871) 3,358,613.

POPULATION OF THE PRINCIPAL TOWNS, ACCORDING TO THE CENSUS OF 1871.

Town	Pop.	Town	Pop.
Aberdeen	88,125	Jedburgh	3,322
Airdrie	13,487	Kelso	4,563
Alloa	6,823	Kilmarnock	22,952
Annan	3,170	Kilwinning	7,375
Arbroath	19,974	Kirkcaldy	12,422
Ayr	17,851	Kirkcudbright	3,328
Banff	7,439	Kirkwall	3,434
Brechin	7,933	Lanark	5,099
Campbeltown	6,628	Largs	4,083
Coatbridge	18,708	Leith	44,277
Cupar (Fife)	5,105	Linlithgow	3,689
Dingwall	2,125	Melrose	1,414
Dumbarton	11,414	Millport	1,541
Dumfries	15,435	Montrose	14,548
Dunbar	3,311	Motherwell	5,291
Dundee	118,974	Musselburgh	7,506
Dunfermline	14,958	Nairn	4,220
Dysart	8,920	Oban	2,413
Edinburgh	196,500	Paisley	48,257
Elgin	7,339	Peebles	2,185
Falkirk	9,547	Perth	25,580
Forfar	11,031	Peterhead	8,585
Forres	3,959	Port-Glasgow	10,805
Galashiels	9,678	Portobello	5,481
Glasgow	477,144	Renfrew	4,162
Gourock	3,082	Rothesay	7,760
Greenock	57,138	Rutherglen	9,451
Haddington	4,004	St. Andrews	6,316
Hamilton	11,496	Selkirk	4,640
Hawick	11,355	Stirling	14,276
Helensburgh and Row	3,054	Stranraer	5,939
Inverary	1,001	Tain	1,765
Inverness	14,463	Wick	8,132
Irvine	6,866		

The seven most populous towns are :—1. Glasgow, 477,144; 2. Edinburgh, 196,500 ; 3. Dundee, 118,974 ; 4. Aberdeen, 88,125 ; 5. Greenock, 57,138 ; 6. Paisley, 48,257 ; 7. Leith, 44,277.

EDINBURGH.

HOTELS.—ROYAL; EDINBURGH; BALMORAL; WINDSOR; CALEDONIAN; CLARENDON; PALACE; WATERLOO; CAFÉ ROYAL; RUTLAND; LONDON.
Temperance—WAVERLEY; COCKBURN; DARLING'S.
Private—ALEXANDRA; GUNN'S; ROXBURGHE, etc.

THE Metropolis of Scotland is situated in the county of Mid-Lothian, about two miles from the Firth of Forth. It is built upon several eminences, and, from its resemblance to the ancient capital of Greece, has been styled *The Modern Athens*. The Castle may be likened to the Acropolis, the Calton Hill to the Museum Hill, and, as Dr. Smith remarks in his Classical Dictionary, we have in Arthur's Seat the Hill of St. George, a lofty insulated mountain, with a conical peaked summit, forming the most striking feature in the environs.

The city is divided into two parts—old and new—the former being remarkable for its picturesque irregularity, and the latter for its symmetrical proportions. Besides its natural beauties, many of the localities both within and around it are remarkable for their historical associations; others have been invested with equal interest by the writings of Sir Walter Scott.

PRINCES STREET.

Princes Street is the principal street in Edinburgh, and the one in which most of the hotels are situated. It extends for a mile in a straight line from east to west, and, being built only upon one side, has the character of a terrace. The first object which here attracts the eye is the elegant Gothic spire erected as a monument to the memory of Sir Walter Scott. The architect of this ingenious structure was George M. Kemp, who died before the work was finished. It was completed in 1844 at a cost of £15,000. In the canopy is placed a marble statue of

B

Scott, by Sir John Steell, and a stair of 287 steps conducts to
the summit, which is 200 feet above the level of the street.
Scott was born at Edinburgh, 15th August 1771, and died at
Abbotsford, 21st September 1832.

In this east garden stand bronze statues of Dr. Livingstone,
Adam Black, and Professor Wilson (Christopher North). West
of the Royal Institution there are a marble statue of *Allan
Ramsay*, the Scottish poet, a bronze figure of the late Sir James
Simpson, and a memorial cross to the late Dean Ramsay.

The Royal Institution and National Gallery.

The Royal Institution standing between the two gardens is a
classical building, designed by the late W. H. Playfair,
surrounded with long ranges of pillars, and with a portico filled
with columns. It contains

The Antiquarian Museum.

which is open to the public on the following terms :—On Tuesday, Wednesday, and Saturday, from 10 to 4, also on Saturday
evening, from 7 to 9, free ; and on Thursday and Friday at the
same hours on payment of 6d. each.

This Museum contains the most extensive and interesting collection of British and Foreign antiquities in Scotland. The
former consist of STONE IMPLEMENTS (Celts' axe, arrow, and
spear heads, stones from vitrified forts, and articles found in Picts'
houses, tumuli, etc.) ; SEPULCHRAL REMAINS (human crania from
early graves, clay and stone urns, etc.) ; BRONZE IMPLEMENTS
(axe-heads, swords, daggers, etc.) ; PERSONAL ORNAMENTS of
gold, silver, and bronze ; SCULPTURED STONES, and miscellaneous
curiosities of later date, such as Rob Roy's *purse*, with concealed
pistols ; *the Thumbikins*, and other well-known Scotch instru-
ments of torture, much used against the Covenanters ; *the
Maiden*, or Scotch guillotine ; an abundance of Roman Catholic
remains, including the beautiful old bell of Kilmichael Glassrie ;
John Knox's pulpit from St. Giles' Church ; and *Jenny Geddes's
stool*, which she hurled at the Dean of St. Giles on his attempt-
ing to read the service-book ; copies of the *Covenant ;* and the
Solemn League and Covenant, with the subscription of Archbishop Leighton ; one of the *banners of the Covenant* borne by
the Covenanters at the battle of Bothwell Brig ; the *blue ribbon*

worn by Prince Charles as a Knight of the Garter when in Scotland in 1745; and a parting *ring* given to him by Flora Macdonald. Among the interesting Roman remains there may be seen a Sculptured Slab, found at Bridgeness, Linlithgowshire, where the Roman wall is supposed to have terminated on the east, with an inscription recording the erection of so many paces of the wall of Antoninus, and on each side an *alto rilievo.*

The Sculpture Gallery, contained in the same building, consists of a collection of casts from the best ancient works, with some of modern date, and the Albacini Collection of busts of celebrated Greeks and Romans. It is open to the public on Wednesdays and Fridays, from 12 to 4, on payment of 6d., and on Saturday from 10 to 4 free.

THE NATIONAL GALLERY OF PAINTING, situated a little above the Royal Institution, is open to the public *free* each day of the week from 10 to 4, except Thursday, Friday, and Sunday. On Thursday and Friday the admission fee is 6d. This building, somewhat in the same style of architecture, was founded in 1850 by the late Prince Albert, and finished in 1854. It contains a select collection of ancient and modern pictures, including some noble specimens of Vandyck, Titian, Tintoretto, Velasquez, Paul Veronese, Guido, Francesco Albano, Spagnoletto, Rembrandt, and others; also some very fine portraits by Sir Thomas Lawrence, Sir Henry Raeburn, Sir John Watson Gordon, and Mr. Graham Gilbert. One of the rooms is devoted to modern art, including paintings by Sir Noel Paton, Erskine Nicol, Douglas, Faed, Herdman; and the late Sir George Harvey, Drummond, John Philip, Horatio M'Culloch, Lauder, W. B. Johnstone, Dyce, Etty, Roberts, and others. Several very fine paintings have been bequeathed to the institution privately, among which are the celebrated portrait of Mrs. Graham, by Gainsborough, and some beautiful works of Jean Baptiste Greuze.

The small but fine collection of water-colours (in the south room) embraces some beautiful works by "Grecian" Williams, and specimens of Girten, Cox, Collins, Cattermole, Lewis, Roberts, Nash, Prout, and Cristall. Among the few works of sculpture is Flaxman's beautiful statue of Burns.

At the west end of Princes Street is ST. JOHN'S EPISCOPAL CHAPEL, an elegant structure of the florid Gothic order. On the open space at the end of the chancel a monumental cross has been erected to the memory of the late Dean Ramsay, who was for many years incumbent of the church. In one of the vaults of the Chapel Sir William Hamilton is interred. The West Churchyard is surrounded by an extensive burying-ground, in which lies Thomas De Quincey, the English Opium-Eater. Turning to the north, a few steps will conduct the stranger to Charlotte Square, in the centre of which stands the SCOTTISH NATIONAL MEMORIAL to the late PRINCE ALBERT, an Equestrian statue with bas-reliefs on the pedestal, by Sir John Steell, R.S.A., who received the honour of knighthood on the occasion of its inauguration by the Queen. The surrounding groups are by other artists. On the west side of the Square is ST. GEORGE'S CHURCH, the handsomest place of worship in the Scotch Establishment, built after the model of St. Paul's, London.

Passing through the lane by the side of this church, the stranger will proceed by Randolph Crescent to the DEAN BRIDGE, a construction of the late Mr. Telford's, which spans the Water of Leith, and commands a fine view. At its farther extremity is Trinity Episcopal Church. About a quarter of a mile to the westward of this (off the Queensferry Road) * is THE DEAN CEMETERY, situated on a steep bank of the Water of Leith, where some of the distinguished men of Edinburgh are interred, including Lords Jeffrey, Cockburn, Rutherfurd, Murray, Professor Wilson, and Alexander Russel. A little beyond the Dean Cemetery is Stewart's Hospital.

Retracing our way to Randolph Crescent, we pass to Great Stuart Street, and Ainslie and Moray Places, a series of elegant streets and squares. Thence we reach St. Colme Street, at the corner of which a chaste Eleanor Cross has been erected in honour the late Miss Catherine Sinclair, authoress of *Modern*

---

* THE FETTES COLLEGE, situated at Comely Bank, forms a conspicuous object in the view from Queensferry Road, from which it is easily accessible. The institution was endowed by the late Sir William Fettes, and consists of a college for the education of boys. The building, which is exceedingly handsome, was designed by David Bryce, R.S.A.

Accomplishments, and to whom Edinburgh is indebted for numerous drinking fountains.

Proceeding eastward, the first opening on the right is North Castle Street, where may be seen the house (No. 39) occupied by Sir Walter Scott during the most interesting period of his life, 1800 to 1826.

The more western district of Edinburgh embraces some fine streets, including Melville Street, Chester Street, Manor Place, Grosvenor and Lansdowne Crescents, and Palmerston Place.

St. Mary's Cathedral.

The vista of Melville Street is closed on the west by the modern pile of St. Mary's Cathedral. This magnificent structure is the result of a bequest by two ladies (Misses Walker of Coates) to the Scottish Episcopal Church and clergy. The architect was the late Sir Gilbert Scott, who adopted the cruciform plan and Early Pointed style. At the intersection of the choir and transepts rises the central tower and spire to the height of 295 feet, including the cross on the summit. The external dimensions of the building are 262 × 67 feet. The two towers above the beautiful west entrance from Palmerston Place, and chapter-house, are still unfinished. Exclusive of these, the cost has already reached £110,000. The interior is beautifully finished, and there is a fine peal of bells in the tower.

Farther west in the same direction is Donaldson's Hospital, a noble building, designed by the late W. H. Playfair, architect, for the purpose of a charitable institution. The founder was a printer, who bequeathed his fortune (£200,000) for the maintenance and education of a limited number of poor and deaf and dumb children.

REGISTER OFFICE AND POST-OFFICE.

At the eastern termination of Princes Street stands the Register Office, which serves as the depository for the public registers and records of Scotland. In front of the building is placed Sir John Steell's equestrian statue of the Duke of Wellington. The General Post and Telegraph Office is a handsome commodious

building on the opposite side of the street, the *Poste Restante*
and Strangers' Inquiry Office being to the left on entrance.   The
Sunday delivery of letters takes place by personal application,
from 8 to 9 A.M. at the General Post-Office.

THE THEATRE-ROYAL

is situated in Broughton Street, next to St. Mary's Roman
Catholic Church, about five minutes' walk from the Post-Office
by Leith Street.   The Box-office of this theatre, as well as the
Princess's, is at Messrs. Wood and Co., 49 George Street.   Per-
formances commence at 7.30.

Proceeding due east from Princes Street, we enter WATERLOO
PLACE, where are situated the OFFICES OF THE INLAND' RE-
VENUE, the Waterloo and Waverley Temperance Hotels.   A
little beyond the latter is the Calton burying-ground, containing
the plain circular monument to David Hume the historian, and
obelisk erected to the memory of the *political martyrs*, Muir,
Palmer, Skirving, Gerrold, and Margarot, who were banished
for their revolutionary opinions in 1794.   Immediately to the
east of the churchyard is the Edinburgh Prison.

CALTON HILL.

The Calton Hill, one of the most marked features of Edinburgh, is approached from Waterloo Place by a flight of steps,
nearly opposite the Prison, in mounting which we pass on the
left the classical monument erected to the late Dugald Stewart.
Close by is the Royal Observatory, adjoining which is a monument
to the late Professor Playfair, the mathematician.   Upon the
summit stands NELSON'S MONUMENT, the top of which may be
reached by a circular stair.   It is 350 feet above the level of the
sea, and commands an extensive panoramic view, and such as
is rarely obtained in a large city.   Looking westwards, the eye
is carried along the vista of Princes Street to the Corstorphine
Hills.   To the south are the crowded and dingy buildings of the
Old Town, covering the ridge that slopes from the Castle to Holyrood.   Over this grim assemblage of roofs and chimneys broods
a cloud of smoke, from which the town acquired the name of
" Auld Reekie."   To the north lie the New Town and the seaports of Leith and Granton.   The monument now serves the use-

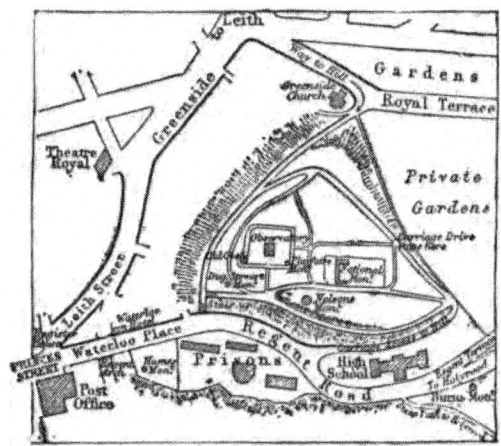

PLAN OF CALTON HILL.

ful purpose of a time-signal, a ball falling simultaneously with the firing of a gun from the Castle.

THE NATIONAL MONUMENT, another classical structure on the Calton Hill, was built to commemorate the heroes who fell at Waterloo. The design is a reproduction of the Parthenon, but unfortunately the ambition of the projectors was in advance of their funds, and it remains unfinished. On the southern slope of the hill is THE HIGH SCHOOL, the principal public seminary of Edinburgh; and on the opposite side of the Regent Road stands BURNS'S MONUMENT, containing a number of letters of the poet, an excellent bust by Wm. Brodie, R.S.A., and some relics.

Returning from the eastern part of Edinburgh to Princes Street, we now conduct the stranger by St. Andrew Street into

ST. ANDREW SQUARE,

one of the principal places of business in the city, and where, or in the immediate vicinity of which, most of the banks and insurance offices are situated. The column which occupies the

centre was erected in 1821 to the memory of the famous Lord
Melville, who was impeached for culpable laxity in transactions
relating to public money, but acquitted by the House of Lords.
It is 136 feet in height. In the north-west corner of the square
(No. 21, third floor) Lord Brougham was born; and the house
directly opposite, in the south-west corner, was David Hume's.
In the centre of the east side of the square, standing apart from
the other buildings, is the *Royal Bank*, having in front an
equestrian statue of the fourth Earl of Hopetoun. The adjoining *British Linen Company's Bank* has a frontage of isolated
Corinthian columns, and the large polished pillars of the telling-
room are of solid granite. The offices of the Scottish Widows'
Fund and Scottish Provident Institution are also in this square,
and are worthy of inspection.

In this locality (east end of Queen Street) are the EDINBURGH
PHILOSOPHICAL INSTITUTION, containing newsroom and library,
the hall of the ROYAL COLLEGE OF PHYSICIANS, and the CALE-
DONIAN UNITED SERVICE CLUB.

From St. Andrew Square we emerge into

GEORGE STREET,

the second in importance after Princes Street, to which it
runs parallel. George Street, although rather uniform in its
style, is remarkable both for its breadth and length, the latter
being exactly half-a-mile. About the centre of the eastmost
division is ST. ANDREW'S CHURCH; and on the opposite side the
Commercial Bank of Scotland, the handsome vestibule and
spacious telling-room of which are worthy of notice. THE
ASSEMBLY ROOMS and MUSIC HALL, where the public balls and
concerts of Edinburgh mostly take place, is an externally plain
building, ornamented by a portico, and situated in a central
part of this street. A little farther west, on the same side, is
the new building of the *Union Bank of Scotland*. At the three
main intersections of this street there have been erected statues
of George IV., William Pitt, and Dr. Chalmers.

At the foot of Pitt Street, which descends in a straight line
from George Street and Hanover Street, is the ROYAL PATENT
GYMNASIUM, a large arena devoted to athletic sports. It contains a patent safety swimming-bath, skating-pond, velocipede
course, and other appliances for exercise and recreation.

OLD TOWN.

THE CASTLE—WEST BOW—HIGH STREET—OLD HOUSES—ST. GILES'S CHURCH—
PARLIAMENT HOUSE—ROYAL EXCHANGE—KNOX'S HOUSE—CANONGATE—
HOLYROOD—ARTHUR'S SEAT AND QUEEN'S DRIVE—UNIVERSITY—HERIOT'S
HOSPITAL.

THE old town of Edinburgh is separated from the new by a wide valley, now laid out as gardens and intersected by the railway. This valley is crossed at three points : first, by an artificial mound opposite Hanover Street ; second, by Waverley Bridge ; and at the General Post Office by the North Bridge. By either of these we obtain access to the High Street of Edinburgh, by which we approach the Castle.

EDINBURGH CASTLE, the original nucleus round which the city grew, is built upon a precipitous rock, 383 feet above the level of the sea. Before the invention of gunpowder it was considered almost impregnable ; but now its strength is more apparent than real. The buildings are principally modern, and consist of barracks for 2000 soldiers, and an armoury for 30,000 stand of arms. The principal or Half-moon Battery faces the north-east, and is mounted with guns of various sizes, which are fired on holidays and festive occasions.

Much historical interest is attached to the old fortress, and it has been the scene of various daring exploits. One of these, as related by Sir Walter Scott in his *Tales of a Grandfather*, had for its object the recovery of the castle from the English in 1313, by a midnight attack. The perilous expedition was undertaken by thirty men, commanded by Randolph, Earl of Moray, guided by Francis, one of his own soldiers. The darkness of the night, the steepness of the precipice, the danger of discovery by the watchmen, and the slender support which they had to trust to in ascending from crag to crag, rendered the enterprise such as might have appalled the bravest spirit. When they had ascended half-way, they found a flat spot large enough to halt upon, and there sat down to recover their breath, and prepare for scaling the wall. This they effected by means of a ladder which they had brought with them. Ere they had all mounted, however, the sentinels caught the alarm, raised the cry of "Treason!" and the constable of the castle and others rushing to the spot, made a gallant but ineffectual resistance. The Earl of Moray was for some time in great personal danger, until the gallant constable was slain, when his followers fled or fell before the hands of the assailants.

The castle esplanade supplies a convenient space for drill, and the parapet wall on the south commands an extensive view of the southern districts of Edinburgh, including Heriot's Hospital, the Grassmarket, and Pentland Hills.

Crossing, from this, the moat by the drawbridge, we pass through the old *Portcullis Gate*, and underneath the ancient *State Prison* in which the Marquis and Earl of Argyle, and numerous adherents of the Stuarts, were confined previous to their trial and execution. Beyond this, on the left, a steep narrow staircase leads directly to the Crown-room. But, following the carriage-road, we pass on the right the Argyle Battery, and a little farther, on the same side, the *Armoury*, behind which is the *Old Sallyport*, next the prison and St. Margaret's Chapel. We then reach the old Palace yard, containing the *Crown Room*, in which are deposited

The Regalia,

Admittance free daily from 11 to 3 P.M.

the insignia of Scottish royalty, consisting of a crown, a sceptre, sword of state, and Lord-Treasurer's rod of office. These "honours of Scotland," as they were called, have a very interesting history;* and, as Sir Walter Scott remarks, we cannot wonder at the fond desire which Scottish antiquaries have shown to refer their date, in the language of national song, to

> "Days when gude KING ROBERT rang."

And although no direct proof can be produced that this was actually the case, there are circumstances which render the conjecture highly probable.

The sceptre, the touch of which gave the Royal assent, performed its last grand legislative office by ratifying the treaty of Union with England on the 16th of January 1707. The Earl of Seafield, then chancellor, on returning it to the clerk, is

---

* See Scott's *Provincial Antiquities.*

reported to have scornfully applied the vulgar phrase, *"There is an end of an auld sang."*

Adjoining the Crown-room, but having a separate entrance from the square, is

QUEEN MARY'S ROOM,

a small apartment on the ground-floor, at the south-east corner of this wing of the quadrangle. Here Queen Mary gave birth to James VI., in whom the crowns of England and Scotland were united. On the wall is an inscription, surmounted by the Scottish arms and the date 19th IVNII, 1566. *Queen Margaret's Chapel,* so named after the Saxon princess, queen of Malcolm Canmore, is situated on the highest part of the Castle rock. This building was long used as a powder-magazine, and its antiquity and interest were unheeded, until attention was drawn to it as a relic of Norman architecture. It was then restored (1853) under the superintendence of Mr. Billings.

Close by are the Bomb Battery and Mons Meg, the latter being a gigantic piece of artillery made at Mons, in Belgium, in 1476, coopered of thick iron bars, hooped together, and about 20 inches diameter in the bore. The Bomb Battery is one of the finest points from which to obtain a view of Edinburgh.

ROUTE FROM THE CASTLE DOWN THE HIGH STREET TO HOLYROOD.

Retracing our steps to the Esplanade, we commence a gradual descent down the the High Street to Holyrood. This street (though generally named High Street) is divided into five portions—viz. "The Castle Hill;" "The Lawnmarket" (Linen-market); "The High Street;" "Netherbow;" and "Canon-gate."

On leaving the Esplanade an opening on the left conducts to Ramsay Gardens, so named after Allan Ramsay, the Scottish poet, and author of the *Gentle Shepherd,* whose house, now called Ramsay Lodge, stands detached to the west of the street. Here the poet died in the year 1757. In Ramsay Lane may be seen the Original Ragged School, associated with the name and benevolent exertions of the Rev. Dr. Guthrie.* We next pass

* The United Industrial School, another similar institution, is in Black-friars Street.

The Assembly Hall,

the meeting-place of the General Assembly of the Church of Scotland, with an elegant spire 241 feet in height, nearly opposite which is the Free Church Assembly Hall.

Immediately facing the entrance to the Assembly Hall there existed, until recently taken down, a remnant of the West Bow, which, some hundred years ago, contained the Assembly Rooms, and was the principal avenue to the more elevated streets of the city. In this alley stood the House of Major Weir, the notorious wizard, who, along with his sister, suffered death for witchcraft in 1670. The West Bow has been superseded by Victoria Street, which leads down to the Grassmarket, a place of some antiquity, although now modernised. It used to be the place for public executions, and here Porteous (who figures in Scott's "Heart of Midlothian") was hanged by the mob from a dyer's pole. A spacious corn-market now occupies part of the south side of the area.

A little farther down, on the left (north) side of the Lawn-market, is James's Court (erected about 1725-27), containing the first residence of David Hume the historian, and of Boswell the biographer of Johnson. The houses of Edinburgh were then, and many still are, divided into *flats* (floors), with separate entrances from one common stair. It was to this flat that Boswell brought Johnson, in 1773, before starting on his tour to the Hebrides.

At the termination of the Lawnmarket, Bank Street diverges on the north, and George IV. Bridge on the south, the first affording an access to Princes Street by the Mound, and taking its name from the Bank of Scotland, situated here, the principal and oldest bank in Scotland.

At this point of the street we enter the Parliament Square, in the midst of which stands

St. Giles's Church,

the church of the Patron Saint, and ancient parish-church of Edinburgh, and, next to the Castle and Holyrood, the most interesting building in Edinburgh for its historical associations. Architecturally, it contains many fine features, which have recently been rescued from the incumbrances of a barbarous age. The choir and southern section have been restored, and an effort is being made to open up the whole building and restore it as far as possible to its original condition. The spire, in the form, of an octagonal lantern, has fortunately been untouched, and exhibits those irregularities found in the finest specimens of Gothic work. On the 13th October 1643 the Solemn League and Covenant was sworn to and subscribed within its walls by the Committee of Estates of Parliament, the Commission of the Church, and the English Commission. The Regent Moray and the Marquis of Montrose were interred near the centre of the south transept, and on the outside of its northern wall is the monument of Napier of Merchiston, the inventor of logarithms. The judges and magistrates attend divine service here in their official robes.

Within the railing, near the entrance, may be seen the Shaft of the Old Cross of Edinburgh. At the north-west corner formerly stood the Old Tolbooth gaol, commonly called "The Heart of Mid-Lothian," rendered famous by Scott's novel of that name. The site is indicated by the figure of a heart in the pavement of the crossing.

The ground now occupied by Parliament Square was originally the ancient cemetery of St. Giles's Church, where many notable men were interred, including John Knox, whose grave is marked by a stone inserted in the pavement, near the statue of Charles II., and inscribed I. K. 1572. The equestrian statue of Charles II. is a well-executed work in lead, representing the monarch in the Roman dress.

THE PARLIAMENT HOUSE

has been appropriated since the time of the Union for the meeting of the Supreme Courts. It was erected between the years 1632 and 1640, but subsequently, with the exception of the great hall, almost totally renewed. The entrance to the courts is at the south-west angle of the square, and the tourist is free to enter. The great hall (122 feet by 49, with a lofty roof of carved oak) was finished in 1639 for the Scottish Parliament, and was thus used until the Union. It now serves as the waiting-room of the advocates and other practitioners in the

Courts, and is ornamented with statues and portraits of distinguished lawyers, and with several windows of stained glass. *The
Stained Glass Window* which has been filled into the south side
of the hall, represents the inauguration of the Court by the
youthful James V. in 1537.

The Lords Ordinary sit in small court-rooms entering from
below this window, called the Outer House. Adjoining them
are two larger courts appropriated to the use of the Inner House,
and called the First and Second Divisions. Adjoining the court-
rooms of the Divisions is another of nearly similar appearance,
in which sits the High Court of Justiciary, the supreme criminal
tribunal of Scotland. Connected with the Parliament House,
and entered from the hall, is

The Advocates' Library,

one of the five entitled to a copy of every book published in
Great Britain, and containing the most valuable collection of
books and manuscripts in Scotland.

The western wing of the Parliament Square is formed by the
Signet Library and County Hall. The former is peculiarly rich
in its archæological department, more especially in British and
Irish history ; the latter is the place for meetings connected
with the county. The eastern wing is formed by the Exchequer
Chambers and Police Office. The City Chambers or Municipal
Offices are situated nearly opposite the Parliament House, and
form part of a building called the Royal Exchange. Here the
business of the Magistrates and Town-Council is carried on. At
No. 11 orders of admission to Heriot's Hospital are granted.

Proceeding downwards, we pass the head of Cockburn Street,
then cross the line of the North and South Bridges at the Tron
Church, and a little farther down we reach

John Knox's House,

Open Wednesdays and Saturdays from 10 to 4—admission 6d.
(Tickets at shop below.)

the dwelling provided for the Scottish Reformer, and where he
resided from the year 1560 until his death in 1572. The house,
as now shown, consists of three rooms—the sitting-room, bedroom, and study. The old oak panelling, though not the

original lining, is wood of a similar description, taken from
other old houses in Edinburgh. The interior affords a specimen
of an old Scotch dwelling-house of the 16th century.

At this point of the street the Canongate commences, extending downwards to Holyrood. This narrow street was once
the main avenue from the palace into the city, and here many
of the ancient nobility of Scotland had their residences.
MORAY HOUSE, on the south side of the street, was the ancient
mansion of the Earls of Moray, and is now used as the Free
Church Normal School.

The Canongate Tolbooth or Court-House, on the north side
of the street, was erected in the reign of James VI., and is a
good specimen of the French style of architecture adopted in
Scotland. In the churchyard of the *Canongate Church* (a large
square building on the same side) are interred Adam Smith, the
author of *The Wealth of Nations,*—Dugald Stewart, David
Allan the artist, and Ferguson the poet.

We next pass the Abbey Court-House and Debtors' Sanctuary,
and then emerge into the open space in front of Holyrood
Palace, having in its centre an elegant fountain, which was
erected by the late Prince Albert.

HOLYROOD PALACE.

Open at 11 A.M. every day, except Sunday. Admission by ticket, sold
within the quadrangle, price sixpence.—Saturdays free.

This venerable seat of Scottish royalty, as is still expressed in
its ordinary name, The Abbey, was originally a convent, and,
like so many other monastic establishments, calls David I. its
founder.

It was nearly wholly rebuilt by Charles II., who showed a
liberal attention to the condition of his ancient metropolis. The
building is in the French style of Louis XIV.'s reign, in the
form of a quadrangle, built around a central court surrounded
with piazzas. The front is two storeys high, and flat on the
roof, closing the inner court as with a screen, and giving access
to it under a handsome cupola, surmounted by an imperial
crown executed in stone work. At each angle of the front the
building projects and rises above the line, being decorated with
turrets at the angles.

The Picture Gallery is the largest apartment in the palace, and on its walls are suspended a number of fanciful portraits of Scottish kings, from which must be excepted an interesting portrait of Mary Queen of Scots, and another representing James III. and his queen, Margaret of Denmark.

Among the portraits in Lord Darnley's rooms is one of the youthful Lord Darnley and his brother. It may be observed that Lord Darnley had access from these rooms to the private stair communicating with the Queen's above. The TAPESTRY ROOM contains two large pieces of ancient tapestry, a portrait of James, fourth Duke of Hamilton, and other paintings.

QUEEN MARY'S APARTMENTS are the most ancient in the palace, and remain an interesting relic of the unhappy Princess by whom they were occupied. Passing through the Audience Chamber, we enter the Queen's Bedroom, with some antique furniture. The roof of this, as of the previous room, is divided into panels, on which are painted various initials and coats-of-arms. The interest of this room hangs on its connection with the tragical murder of the favourite, Riccio, the story of which forms so romantic an episode in Scottish history. The act, as related, was accomplished by the Queen's husband, Darnley, and a number of conspirators, who, entering by a secret passage, took the Queen and her party by surprise. The door of this secret approach, and the adjoining cabinet or closet where the conspirators found their victim, may still be seen. Riccio is said to have been dragged from this to the door of the Audience Chamber, where he was finally despatched, and the spot where the body lay is still marked by a blood-stain upon the floor.

After visiting Queen Mary's apartments, the tourist descends the staircase and proceeds to the Chapel-Royal, being a fragment of the ancient

Abbey of Holyrood House,

founded (as already mentioned) in 1128 by David I. The fragment which remains forms the nave of the ancient building, and among the additions of a later age may be traced remnants of the original work of the 12th century. The west front, although partly the work of different periods, is on the whole in the most beautiful style of Early English, and its sculptured arcade, boldly-cut heads, and rich variety of ornament in the doorway, are much admired. The windows above are additions of the time of Charles I., whose initials appear below. The nave was fitted up by this monarch as a chapel-royal, that it might serve as a model of the Episcopal worship, which he was anxious to introduce into Scotland, and he was himself crowned here in 1633. In the belfry tower, at the N.E. corner, is a marble monument to Lord Belhaven (1639), well executed, and other members of the Scottish nobility have tombs in different places. In the south-east corner is the royal vault, in which are deposited the remains of David II., James II., James V. and Magdalen his queen, Lord Darnley, and other illustrious members of the royal line. Riccio's grave is in the passage leading from the quadrangle to the Abbey.

ARTHUR'S SEAT,

which rises immediately above Holyrood, is encircled by an excellent carriage-road called "The Queen's Drive," from which beautiful and varied views are obtained. Those who prefer to climb the mountain side may do so conveniently from Holyrood by crossing the park, and then taking the direction of St. Anthony's Chapel, or by the road, along the Salisbury Crags. An easier mode of ascent is to follow the Queen's Drive to Dunsappie Loch, and from thence strike up the hill to the summit, which is 822 feet above the level of the sea, and commands an extensive view.

St. ANTHONY'S CHAPEL, the ruins of which form so picturesque an object on the shoulder of the hill, belonged originally to the cell of a hermit. A high rock rises behind the cell, from the foot of which gushes a pure and plentiful fountain, dedicated to Saint Anthony, the *genius loci*. The spot is interesting from its association with some of the incidents in Scott's "Heart of Mid-Lothian ;" and particularly as the scene where Jeanie Deans met the ruffian Robertson.

Duddingston Loch and village lie at the foot of the south-east portion of Arthur's Seat. In the village of Duddingston may still be seen the house in which Prince Charles Stuart slept before the battle of Prestonpans. In the vicinity, also, are Duddingston House, a seat of the Abercorn family, and Prestonfield House, the seat of Sir W. H. Dick Cunyngham, Bart. The road at this part of the hill is overhung by

c

a range of porphyritic greenstone columns of a pentagonal or hexagonal form, from 50 to 60 feet in length, and 5 in diameter, called Samson's Ribs. We re-enter the town by the park-keeper's lodge near St. Leonard's Hill, where Jeanie Deans' cottage may still be seen.

THE UNIVERSITY.

THE UNIVERSITY of Edinburgh occupies a central position in the street named after the South Bridge, and on a site historically famous as the scene of the tragical death of Darnley. It may conveniently be visited on the way from Holyrood or Arthur's Seat. It dates its existence from the reign of James VI., in the year 1582. The first professor was appointed in 1583; and about the year 1660, by means of benefactions from public bodies and private individuals, the University had attained a respectable rank among similar institutions. As a school of medicine it first rose into repute under Dr. Alexander Monro, who became professor of anatomy in 1720; and in this branch of science it afterwards attained a distinguished pre-eminence from possessing professors remarkable for their abilities and success as teachers. In the other branches of knowledge its reputation was gradually exalted by Maclaurin, Black, Ferguson, Stewart, Robinson, and other eminent men. The present building was commenced in 1789, after a plan by Mr. Robert Adam, and subsequently finished in conformity with a design furnished by the late W. H. Playfair, in the form of a parallelogram. The entrance is by a massive portico, supported by four large Doric columns, each consisting of one solid hewn stone, and bearing a Latin inscription, which records the various dates of the foundation and building. On the left of the quadrangle on entrance is the library, which is shown to the public, by an attendant, for a small fee; and at the farther extremity a statue of the late Sir David Brewster, who at his death was Principal of the College.

Contiguous with the University, though in a different style of architecture, is THE MUSEUM OF SCIENCE AND ART, which is open daily, except Sundays. The entrance is from Chambers Street, and the terms of admission are as follows :—*Free* on Wednesday, Friday, and Saturday, from 10 A.M. till 4 P.M., and on Friday and Saturday evenings from 6 to 9. *Pay Days*—Monday, Tuesday, and Thursday, from 10 A.M. till 4 P.M., 6d. each. This museum is a branch of the Science and Art department, and resembles Kensington Museum on a smaller scale. The building was designed by the late Captain Fowke, R.E., and is built of fine white Binny stone, relieved by light pilasters of red sandstone. The floor of the Great Saloon is set apart for articles illustrative of the arts of construction. Next in order are placed the cements and stones. About the centre are specimens of large guns and balls.

In the front of the east wing is the lecture-room, behind which is the NATURAL HISTORY SALOON.

Above the lecture-room, in the east wing, there is a fine collection of minerals and fossils, including those which belonged to the late Hugh Miller. *

From the University we pass on to GEORGE IV. BRIDGE, which crosses the Cowgate near its junction with the Grassmarket. Here, on the one hand, stand the HALL OF THE HIGHLAND AND AGRICULTURAL SOCIETY OF SCOTLAND, the parent of the very numerous bodies which now devote special attention to the advancement of agriculture ; and opposite, on the east side, the Sheriff Court-House and Augustine Church, the principal Independent Chapel in Edinburgh. At the southern end of the bridge, on the west, is the GREYFRIARS CHURCH, surrounded by an ancient CHURCHYARD, which was formerly the garden of the monastery. Here some of the most notable Scotsmen are interred, including George Buchanan, the Latin poet and preceptor of James VI. ; Allan Ramsay, the Scottish poet ; Principal Robertson, the historian ; Dr. Black, the chemist ; Dr. Hugh Blair ; Colin Maclaurin ; Dr. M'Crie, the biographer of Knox ; Patrick Fraser Tytler, and others. Of the monuments, the most interesting is that erected to *the martyrs* who were executed for their religious opinions at the time of the Covenanters. The Greyfriars Church is of ancient date, having been built in 1612, and it was here that the first signatures to the National Covenant were appended in 1663. It was destroyed

* Those interested in such sights may, while here, conveniently visit the Museum of THE ROYAL COLLEGE OF SURGEONS, Nicolson Street [open daily, except Tuesday, from 12 to 4, winter 12 to 3] ; and the Phrenological Museum, Surgeon Square, containing a large collection of busts, skulls, and masks. It is open to the public every Saturday afternoon, from 1 to 6 P.M., free of charge ; but strangers may have access any day.

by fire in 1845, and afterwards re-erected, with stained glass windows and an organ. Leaving the churchyard, and advancing along Forrest Road, we reach the New Medical Hall, an elegant building, of which Mr. Anderson is architect. On the other side of the Walk, opposite Heriot's Hospital, stands

The New Infirmary,

a building in the Scottish Baronial style, after a plan by David Bryce, R.S.A., which embodies all the latest improvements in hospital construction, with a capacity of accommodation for 600 patients. The foundation-stone was laid in October 1870 by H.R.H. the Prince of Wales.

Heriot's Hospital.

Admission daily from 12 to 3, Saturdays and Sundays excepted, by ticket obtained at 11 Royal Exchange, High Street.

is one of the finest buildings in Edinburgh. It was founded by George Heriot, jeweller to James VI., whose name will be familiar to readers of Scott's "Fortunes of Nigel." Heriot followed his royal master to London upon the union of the Crowns, and died in 1624, leaving an immense fortune for this charity. The building consists of a quadrangle, with large square towers at each angle. From the north front rises a lofty central tower, adorned by a statue of the founder, under which an archway leads to the inner courts. The south front presents also a circular tower, with Gothic windows, which serve to light a handsome chapel. The average number of boys maintained is 180.

Suburbs.

Edinburgh has the advantage of some beautiful suburbs. Those on the south and south-west comprise the districts of Newington, Grange, Bruntsfield, Morningside, Merchiston. To the west is Murrayfield. The Meadows and Bruntsfield Links are two extensive commons or parks, where golf, cricket, and other games are played. At the Grange is situated the Southern Cemetery, where the late Dr. Chalmers, Hugh Miller, and others, are interred. In the same locality is the old Mansion-house of Grange (now a school), which for a long period was the residence of the late Sir Thomas Dick Lauder, author of the account of the *Morayshire Floods, Highland Rambles*, etc. At Merchiston is Merchiston Castle (now an Academy for boys), where the celebrated Napier, inventor of logarithms, was born about 1550.

The space of ground which extends from Morningside to the bottom of Blackford Hill was formerly called the Borough Moor. Here James IV. arrayed his army previous to his departure for Flodden field (1513). The BORE STONE, in which the royal standard was fixed, is still preserved, and may be seen built into the wall, at the gate of Blackford House.

In this neighbourhood is the HERMITAGE OF BRAID, an old seat of Gordon of Cluny, situated at the bottom of a wooded dell. A delightful walk crosses the Braid Hills from east to west, affording beautiful glimpses of the metropolis and Firth of Forth.

About the middle of Inverleith Row, to the north of the town, is the ROYAL BOTANIC GARDEN, to which there is free admission in summer from 6 A.M. till 6 P.M. ; on Saturday (June, July, and August) till 8 P.M. ; in winter from daylight till dusk. This garden embraces an extent of 17 English acres, and presents every facility for prosecuting the study of botany. The Palmhouse, one of the finest in the kingdom, is 100 feet in length, 57 in breadth, and 70 feet in height, and the Museum contains an extensive and interesting collection of plants.

In the same neighbourhood, and entering from nearly opposite the Botanic Garden, is the EDINBURGH CEMETERY, where the late Sir James Y. Simpson, Bart., the eminent physician, Alexander Smith, the poet, and others, are interred.

LEITH.

Leith, though a separate town, and governed by separate magistrates, may, from its contiguity, be called the seaport of Edinburgh, from the centre of which it is distant about a mile and a half. As a naval station it holds an important place, being the principal port on the east coast of Scotland ; and it carries on a large traffic with the Baltic and other foreign parts. It possesses magnificent docks, and two piers (enclosing the harbour) of immense length, the east being 3530 feet, and the west 3123 feet, which afford delightful and healthful promenades. A ferry-

boat plies between the extremities of the piers, so that the visitor
may go by the one and return by the other (fare ½d.)

The modern streets of Leith are spacious and well built, and
the older are being gradually improved.

The public buildings worthy of notice are—The *Parish
Church of South Leith*, a fine Gothic edifice, built previous to
the year 1496. Nearly opposite this, and entering from Con-
stitution Street, is *St. James' Episcopal Church*, an elegant
Gothic building, containing a fine peal of bells. Some of the
other buildings are, the *Corn Exchange*, where business is trans-
acted daily ; the *Assembly Rooms*, containing a handsome ball-
room and public reading-room, and the *Court-House*, which, for
chasteness of design and neatness of workmanship, is a very
favourable specimen of modern architecture. The *Custom-House*
is in North Leith. The *Parish Church of North Leith* is a handsome though unpretending structure, surmounted by a tasteful
spire ; and the living is one of the best in the Church of Scotland. Leith contains some extensive and elegantly-built flour-
mills ; several breweries ; and shipbuilding is carried on to a
considerable extent.

To the west of Albany Street is the *Fort of Leith*, a military
station for a corps of Royal Artillery. Leith is bounded on the
east by extensive Links, where golf forms a favourite recreation.
Here may be seen the remains of some mounds raised by the
besieging army of Cromwell, in 1560, for planting cannon.

NEWHAVEN,

about half-a-mile to the west of Leith, is a small fishing village,
whose inhabitants are noted as a distinct community, rarely in-
termarrying with any other class. The male inhabitants are
almost all fishermen, and the females (fishwomen) are occupied
in selling the produce of their husbands' industry in the streets
of Edinburgh. There is a small pier, from which numerous
fishing-boats ply daily to the neighbouring fishing grounds.

TRINITY,

adjoining Newhaven, is an agreeable suburb of Edinburgh, laid
out in villa residences, many of which enjoy a delightful sea-
view.

GRANTON,

about half-a-mile to the west of Trinity, is the rival port of Leith. It possesses a fine harbour, and the pier is one of the most elegant low-water piers in the kingdom. Granton is the creation of the Duke of Buccleuch. There is a regular steamboat ferry between this and Burntisland (Fife) in connection with the railway.

PORTOBELLO,

three miles to the east of Edinburgh, is a favourite suburban residence and bathing place, and consists of a number of handsome streets and detached villas. The sands are firm, with a gentle slope, and well adapted for bathing. A Marine Parade is constructed along the shore, and an elegant promenade pier projects across the centre of the beach into the sea. Half-way between Portobello and Edinburgh, by the high road, are Piershill Barracks, used as a cavalry depôt. A little to the north of this is the interesting old Church of *Restalrig*, founded by James III. in honour of the Trinity and Virgin Mary, and endowed by the two succeeding monarchs. Two miles to the east of Portobello is the old town of

MUSSELBURGH,

situated at the mouth of the river Esk, and noted for its extensive links, which are considered the best for golf-playing near Edinburgh, and also used for the Edinburgh Races. Here the Marquis of Hamilton, representing Charles I., met the Covenanting party in 1638. It was near Musselburgh that Oliver Cromwell took up his position in 1650, in order to be near his fleet, and from which he retired to Dunbar. A statue is erected at Musselburgh to the memory of the late Dr. Moir the poet (the Delta of *Blackwood's Magazine*), who was a native of the town. At the east end of Musselburgh is Pinkie House, the seat of Sir Archibald Hope, Bart. This interesting mansion was originally a country seat of the Abbot of Dunfermline; and it was converted into its present shape at the beginning of the 17th century by Alexander Seton, Earl of Dunfermline. "Few of our old mansions (says Mr. Billings)

so completely reward inspection, whether by their beauty or
their novelty." About half-a-mile southward of this, on the
fields now intersected by the railway, the battle of Pinkie was
fought (1547), when the Scottish army was defeated by the
English, commanded by the Earl of Hertford, afterwards Duke of
Somerset. Southward, to the right, is Carberry Hill, where Queen
Mary surrendered to the insurgent nobles in 1567; and three miles
eastwards lies Tranent, in whose vicinity the famous battle of
Prestonpans was fought, 21st September 1745, between the royal
forces under Sir John Cope and the Highland army under Prince
Charles Stuart. The incident forms a striking scene in the novel
of "Waverley." South of the station may be seen Bankton House,
where the celebrated Colonel Gardiner resided, who fell on this
occasion, close beside the wall of the park. A monument has
been erected to his memory near the spot.

Haddingtonshire, which is entered by the railway about a
mile eastwards of Musselburgh, is one of the richest agricultural
districts of Scotland, and contains a number of fine properties,
including Tyninghame (the Earl of Haddington), Yester House
(the Marquis of Tweeddale), Lethington (Lord Blantyre),
Whyttingham (Lady Balfour), Gilmerton (Sir David Kinloch,
Bart.), Dirleton and Archerfield (Right Hon. R. C. Nisbet-
Hamilton), Gosford (the Earl of Wemyss), Luchie (Sir Hew
Dalrymple, Bart.), Balgone (Sir George Grant Suttie, Bart.),
Newbyth (Sir David Baird, Bart.), Smeaton (Sir Thomas Buchan
Hepburn, Bart.), and others.

HADDINGTON,

the county town, is situated on the north bank of the Tyne,
in the centre of the county, eighteen miles east of Edinburgh.
It contains a most interesting Gothic church, whose great tower
and choir are roofless, but the nave is still used as the parish
church. It is alleged that John Knox was born in a house near
this church. On the sea-coast, 8 miles to the north, is the
favourite watering-place of

NORTH BERWICK.

There is a good hotel (The Royal) at the station, and on
the west links The Marine. For the game of golf the links
are much esteemed for their extent. The conical hill called

North Berwick Law, rises 640 feet in height, and commands a fine view. About two miles from the shore is the celebrated BASS ROCK, a precipitous isolated rock, which rises sheer out of the water to the height of 400 feet, and is covered with sea-fowl. It affords a favourite sailing excursion to parties residing here. About two and a half miles eastward, on the coast, stand the picturesque ruins of Tantallon Castle, an old stronghold of the Douglas family, and which, as such, is alluded to in Scott's poem of "Marmion." About ten miles farther eastward, in the same county, is the old seaport town of

DUNBAR,

containing the remains of an old Castle, which is built upon isolated rocks projecting into the sea, at the side of the harbour. Dunbar is a very ancient place, having, as early as 1070, been given by Malcolm Canmore to Patrick, Earl of Northumberland, a princely noble, who fled from England at the Conquest, and who became the progenitor of the Cospatricks, Earls of Dunbar and March. It withstood a memorable siege of six weeks in 1335, on which occasion it was gallantly defended by *Black Agnes*, Countess of March, against the English army under the Earl of Salisbury. In the year 1567 Queen Mary appointed the infamous Bothwell governor of the stronghold ; and here she twice found shelter—once after the murder of Riccio, and a second time when she made her escape from Borthwick Castle in the disguise of a page. After her surrender at Carberry Hill, Dunbar Castle was taken and dismantled by the Regent Murray. It is now the property of the Earl of Lauderdale, who is also superior of the burgh in right of the Earl of March. Dunbar House, an old residence of this nobleman's ancestors, is situated at the end of the High Street, and now occupied as a government barrack. There is a fine harbour, formed at great cost amid the surrounding rocks.

Near the town two battles were fought, in both of which the Scots were defeated—one in 1296, when Baliol engaged the forces of Edward I. ; the other, in 1650, when the Scottish army, under General Lesley, was routed by Oliver Cromwell. The latter is still remembered by the people of Scotland under the opprobrious epithet of the "race of Dunbar," or "Tyesday's chase "—the engagement having taken place on a Tuesday. Cromwell on this occasion took up his residence at *Broxmouth Park*, now a seat of the Duke of Roxburghe, about a mile to the east, the grounds of which are open to the public on Wednesdays.

HAWTHORNDEN.

Admission daily, except Sundays.   Charge, 1s. each.

The narrow glen (remarks Sir Walter Scott) which connects these two celebrated spots is one of those beautiful and sequestered valleys which so often occur in Scotland where they are least expected from the general appearance of the surrounding landscape. The first named is within a few minutes' walk of the Hawthornden Railway Station, and during summer a coach leaves Princes Street for Roslin in the morning, returning in the afternoon. There is no admission to Hawthornden House from the Roslin side, but the tourist may walk through the glen from Roslin to Lasswade by a public foot-path on the left bank of the Esk.

HAWTHORNDEN HOUSE, the classic residence of the poet Drummond, rises from the edge of a cliff which descends precipitously to the river Esk. It is small, and not very convenient, and was repaired in 1638, according to an inscription still extant.

It is impossible (says Scott) to see Hawthornden, and mention its poetical owner, without thinking upon the time when

" Jonson sate in Drummond's social shade "—

a remark having reference to the well-known occasion when Ben Jonson undertook a journey to Scotland on foot, in order to meet the Scottish poet.

On the south side of the house, and so situated as to have contributed in some sort to its defence, stand the ruins of an old tower, the abode of the poet's ancestors ; and save that they enjoyed the benefit of God's daylight, it seems one which cannot have been much more comfortable than the caverns below. Through this lies the entrance to the more modern house ; and the neighbourhood of the rude and ruinous pile adds much to the romance of the whole situation. A seat in the rock near the house is still called the "Cypress-grove," in memory of the treatise on the vanity of human life, which Drummond composed here.

Under the mansion lie those subterranean caves which have excited so much speculation amongst antiquaries. They are simply small apartments, hewn out of the solid rock with much labour, and connected with each other by passages of disproportionate length.

From Hawthornden the tourist may proceed to Roslin by a narrow path along the river's side. On the southern bank are to be seen the Caves of Gorton, which afforded shelter to Sir Alexander Ramsay of Dalhousie, and other Scottish patriots, during the reign of David II.

Roslin.

There are two hotels in the village where dinner or refreshments may be obtained ; also stabling.

The Chapel is closed on Saturdays at 6 P.M., and on Sundays it is open for divine service *only*. Admission-fee for seeing Chapel, 1s.

Sunday services—morning at 12.15 P.M., evening (during summer) at 3.30 P.M.

Roslin Chapel was founded in 1446 by William St. Clair, third Earl of Orkney, and Lord of Roslin, and both on account of its architecture and a romantic interest connected with its history it has long been an object of attraction. In point of style it may be said to be one of the most highly decorated specimens of Gothic architecture in Scotland. The nave is bold and lofty, enclosed, as usual, by side aisles, the pillars and arches of which display a profusion of ornament, particularly observable in the so-called "'Prentice's Pillar." Beneath the chapel lie the Barons of Roslin, all of whom, till the time of James VII., were buried in complete armour. The ruins of ROSLIN CASTLE (admission 6d.) stand upon a peninsular rock overhanging the picturesque glen of the Esk, and are accessible by a bridge of considerable height, thrown over a deep incision in the solid rock. Its origin is involved in obscurity, but it was long the abode of the family of St. Clair. It is now in a very ruinous condition, and is remarkable only for its picturesque position.

The whole valley of the Esk abounds in beautiful scenery, and is studded with ancient mansion-houses—

From that fair dome, where suit is paid   Who knows not Melville's beechy
   By blast of bugle free,   And Roslin's rocky glen, [grove,
To Auchindinny's hazel glade,   Dalkeith, which all the virtues love,
   And haunted Woodhouselee.   And classic Hawthornden?
                    Scott's ballad, '**THE GREY BROTHER.**'

Sir Walter Scott spent some of the happiest years of his early life at LASSWADE, a village in this neighbourhood; and Thomas De Quincey, "The English Opium-Eater," retired hither during his later years.

A beautiful walk of two miles from Lasswade will bring the tourist to

DALKEITH,

the seat of the Duke of Buccleuch and Queensberry, which is situated 6 miles from Edinburgh, and may be reached from thence by rail or coach. At the eastern extremity of the village is the main entrance to the Palace, close to which is the Episcopal chapel of ST. MARY'S, where there is choral service on Sundays at 11 A.M. and 3.30 P.M. The PALACE is a large square structure, surrounded by an extensive park, in which the rivers North and South Esk unite. Strangers are admitted in the absence of the family, on Wednesdays and Saturdays. The gardens of Dalkeith Palace have long been famed for their extent and high state of culture, and are well worthy of a visit.

NEWBATTLE ABBEY, the seat of the Marquis of Lothian, is situated about a mile south-west from Dalkeith, on the northern bank of the South Esk; and DALHOUSIE CASTLE, a seat of the Earl of Dalhousie, is about 2 miles farther up the same stream.

On the way to or from Roslin or Dalkeith the tourist may visit the ruins of Craigmillar Castle, 3 miles south of Edinburgh, conspicuously situated on the top of an eminence. Besides the interest attached to the ruin itself, it is well worth visiting on account of the splendid view it commands.

THE PENTLAND HILLS.

These beautiful green hills, which form so striking an object in the landscape about Edinburgh, may be reached most conveniently by a road proceeding nearly due south from the town, passing through the Morningside suburb, and from thence skirting the edge of the Braid hills. By pursuing the main road along the side of the hills, we pass Woodhouselee, the seat of the

Tytler family. Old Woodhouselee, of which the ruins still exist, was the property of the notorious Hamilton of Bothwellhaugh, the assassin of the Regent Moray.

A little beyond this we reach the vale of Glencorse, where is situated Glencorse House, the seat of the Right Honourable John Inglis, Lord President of the Court of Session. This little valley is watered by the Glencorse or Logan burn, at the head of which is HABBIE'S HOWE, a scene alluded to in Ramsay's poem of the *Gentle Shepherd*, and which forms a favourite resort of picnic parties.

The tourist may agreeably vary his drive to Roslin by returning this way, taking a cross road from Roslin to the hills.

HOPETOUN HOUSE,

the seat of the Earl of Hopetoun, is situated on the banks of the Forth, about a mile to the west of the village of South Queensferry, and 10 miles from Edinburgh. The house is a splendid modern structure with extensive wings. But what forms the greatest attraction is the beauty of the policies, which are laid out with much taste, and the garden is noted for its high culture. From the high terrace-walks which overlook the Firth of Forth a beautiful view is obtained. On a peninsula to the westward may be seen Blackness Castle, now used as a powder-magazine, and on the opposite coast Broomhall, the seat of the Earl of Elgin. On the other (the east) side of Queensferry is Dalmeny Park, the seat of the Earl of Rosebery. Dalmeny House is a modern mansion, surrounded by a park of great beauty.

Five miles distant from North Queensferry lies the interesting town of

DUNFERMLINE.

This ancient town is situated in the south-west district of Fifeshire, 15 miles from Edinburgh by road. It is now a large manufacturing town, engaged in the linen trade, the diapers of Dunfermline being famed for their beauty. In a historical point of view it is interesting as having become the seat of government at an early period, and a favourite residence of the Scottish kings, as commemorated in the ballad of Sir Patrick Spens—

> "The king sits in Dunfermline town,
> Drinking the bluid-red wine."

It contains numerous antiquities, the principal of which are
the castle of Malcolm III., surnamed Canmore (who resided
here in 1057), the Palace, and the Abbey.

The Monastery of Dunfermline was founded by Malcolm, at
the instigation of his Queen, Margaret (grand-daughter of
Edmund Ironside), about the year 1075.   He also erected the
Cathedral Church, which was dedicated to the Holy Trinity,
and appointed to be the common cemetery of the kings of Scotland, in place of Iona.   The Abbey, originally a splendid and
extensive building, was almost entirely destroyed by the English
early in the 14th century.   The Church escaped the merciless
hands of the invaders, but afterwards it fell a sacrifice to the blind
zeal of the early Reformers, who entirely demolished all except
the nave, which they converted into a Presbyterian place of
worship.   A large slab of coarse blue marble, on the east side
of the choir of the Cathedral, marks the spot where Malcolm
and his Queen are buried ; and six large flat stones on the
north-east side of the building are placed over the graves of
Malcolm III., Prince Edward, Edgar, Alexander, and David I.,
Malcolm IV., and Alexander III.   The last sovereign who was
interred at Dunfermline was Robert the Bruce, a king whose
memory is deservedly dear to Scotland.   King Robert died at
Cardross, in Dumbartonshire, 7th June 1329.   In 1818 some
workmen, clearing out the ground for the foundation of the new
church, discovered the royal tomb (in front of the present pulpit
—once the site of the high altar), in which the skeleton of this
monarch was found entire, together with the lead in which his
body was wrapped, and even some fragments of his shroud.   The
fratery still retains an entire window, much admired for its
elegant and complicated workmanship.

On the shore of the Firth of Forth, to the south and west
of Dunfermline, there are several old family residences, among
which may be mentioned Broomhall, the seat of the Earl of
Elgin ; Torrie House, the seat of Mrs. J. H. Erskine Wemyss ;
Culross Abbey, an old seat of the Bruce family ; and Dunimarle
Castle, a seat of the Erskine family.   Near Dunimarle tradition fixes the scene of the murder of Lady Macduff and her
children, as described by Shakspeare, and the site of the Thane
of Fife's Castle is still pointed out.

PEEBLES, MELROSE, AND VALE OF TWEED.

PEEBLES,

the county town of Peeblesshire, is situated on the river Tweed, 27 miles from Edinburgh, and contains a good hotel. It is a favourite station for anglers. At an early period it became an occasional residence of the kings of Scotland, and is the scene of the poem of James I., called *Peblis to the Play*. The principal building is the Chambers Institute, a handsome castellated edifice in the High Street, which was presented to his native town by the well-known publisher of that name, to be used for purposes of social improvement.

In the neighbourhood of Peebles there are a number of fine seats, among which may be named Stobo (Sir Graham Montgomery, Bart.), Dalwick House (Sir J. Nasmyth, Bart.), Haystoun (Sir Robert Hay, Bart.), Netherurd (John White, Esq.), Rachan House (J. Tweedie, Esq.)

The Vale of the Tweed, both above and below Peebles, contained a chain of strong castles to serve as a defence against the incursions of English marauders. *Nidpath Castle*, one of the most entire of these, is situated about a mile west from Peebles, on a rock projecting over the north bank of the Tweed.

Four miles distant, at Lyne, are the remains of a Roman camp. In the vale of Manor, near Peebles, may still be seen the cottage and grave of David Ritchie, the original of Sir Walter Scott's Black Dwarf.

A line of rail connects Peebles with the two manufacturing towns of Innerleithen and Galashiels, by which means the tourist may follow the banks of the Tweed all the way to its junction with the Gala. Thence he may continue his journey to Melrose. About a mile from Innerleithen is *Traquair House*, the seat of the Steuarts, Earls of Traquair, and said to be the oldest inhabited house in Scotland, part of it having been built about 1000 years ago. The house is a fine example of an old Scottish baronial residence, with steep roof and turreted corners. At the head of an avenue, forming the southern approach, there is an old gateway ornamented by figures of the old bears which form the supporters of the family arms. In the neighbourhood are

The Pirn, the seat of the family of Horsburgh, and *The Glen*
(Charles Tennent, Esq)., the scene of "Lucy's Flittin'." About
a mile eastwards is the manufacturing village of Walkerburn;
and two miles below (four from Innerleithen) is Elibank Tower,
famous for the story of "Muckle-mou'd Meg." Nearer to
Galashiels are *Ashiestiel*, once the residence of Sir Walter Scott,
where he wrote parts of the Lay of the Last Minstrel and
Marmion, and *Yair*, the seat of the Pringles of Whytbank.
When nearly opposite Ashiestiel the line leaves the valley of
the Tweed, and crosses over by Clovenfords and Torwoodlee to
the vale of the Gala, joining the Waverley Route a mile above
Galashiels.

GALASHIELS * is situated on the banks of the Gala, a river celebrated by Burns, about a mile above its junction with the Tweed,
and four from Melrose. It is now one of the most thriving
seats of the Scottish woollen manufacture.

Melrose.

This interesting village is situated 37 miles to the south of
Edinburgh, and is easily reached by railway. It contains two
good hotels, where vehicles and refreshments may be obtained:

---

* The county town of *Selkirk* is situated about five miles to the south of
Galashiels, a little below the junction of the Ettrick and Yarrow. It contains several large woollen mills. Close by is *The Haining*, the ancient
family seat of the Pringles of Clifton. There is a coach twice a week
(Tuesday and Saturday) from the County Hotel to St. Mary's Loch, in connection with those from Moffat, which meet at Tibbie Shiels' Inn. In the
neighbourhood are *Philiphaugh* (Sir John Murray, Bart.), *Yair* (Alexander
Pringle, Esq.), and *Bowhill* (the Duke of Buccleuch). Beyond this, on the
north bank of the Yarrow, is the farm of Foulshiels, where Mungo Park,
the African traveller, was born (1771). Looking across to the other side
of the river—

"We pass where Newark's stately tower
Looks out from Yarrow's birchen bower."

The battle of Philiphaugh, between Leslie and Montrose, was fought on the
plain on the northern side of the Ettrick, 13th September 1645.

Those who pursue the coach road up Yarrow to St. Mary's Loch pass the
village of Yarrowford (above which is *Broadmeadows*), Hangingshaw Castle,
Deuchar Tower, the village of Yarrow, and Mount-benger, for some years the
residence of James Hogg, the Ettrick Shepherd. Near this is the Gordon
Arms Inn. About a mile to the south of the inn is the homestead of Altrive
Lake (now called Eldin Hope), where the Ettrick Shepherd resided till his
death (1835). (Distance from Selkirk 12 miles.)

—The George, and Abbey. From the railway station it is only a five minutes' walk to the famous Abbey, founded by David I. at the beginning of the twelfth century, and rebuilt in the reign of Robert the Bruce. The architecture of this beautiful fabric is a mixture of the Flamboyant and florid Gothic, somewhat the same as that exhibited in some of the continental cathedrals. It is remarkable for the beauty and delicacy of its ornamental work, much of which, owing to the hardness of the stone, retains its original sharpness. There is a small fee of 4d. each charged for admission.

The entrance is by a wooden gate, where probably stood the chief or western portal. This admits us to the nave with its two aisles, the latter being divided into small chapels, lighted by richly traceried windows. Externally these windows are supported by buttresses, ornamented with niches, pinnacles, and numerous figures, including the Virgin and Child, and Saint Andrew, the patron saint of Scotland.

The *Transept* is a beautiful portion of the building, having on the right a richly ornamented doorway, above which rises the very perfect south window, a work in the best style of florid tracery. Within the south transept access is given to the triforium galleries and belfry by a small door, over which may be seen a shield with compasses and fleur-de-lis, indicating the profession and nation of John Morow, the master-mason of the Abbey. Within the small aisle opposite are the tombs of Michael Scott the famous wizard, and Sir Ralph Eure or Ivers, the latter of whom was killed at the battle of Ancrum Muir in 1545.

The *Choir*, which is built in the form of a Greek cross, is surmounted by the original fretted stone roof, covered with tracery. On the site of the high altar a small stone indicates the spot where the heart of King Robert the Bruce is interred, while on either side are the tombs of Alexander II., and James, second Earl of Douglas, the hero of Otterbourne. Of the three windows by which it is lighted, the finest is the eastern, 57 feet high by 28 wide, which is divided by four tall mullions, interlaced by tracery of such delicacy that it has been compared to an imitation of wicker work :—

> " Thou would'st have thought some fairy's hand
> 'Twixt poplars straight the osier wand
> In many a freaking knot had twined ;
> Then framed a spell when the work was done,
> And changed the willow wreaths to stone."

D

The finest arches are situated at the north-east end of the church, the piers being composed of clustered shafts with beautifully sculptured capitals, thus alluded to in Scott's *Lay of the Last Minstrel*—

> "The keystone that locks each ribbed aisle,
> Is a fleur-de-lis or a quatrefeuille ;
> The corbels are carved grotesque and grim,
> And the pillars with cluster'd shafts so trim,
> With base and with capital flourish'd around,
> Seem bundles of lances which garlands have bound."

By a Norman doorway in the north transept we are admitted into the *Sacristy*, where repose the remains of Queen Johanna, wife of Alexander II. and sister of Henry III. of England. From this we pass into the *Cloisters* by a door on the north-east end of the nave, being the same through which the monk in the *Lay of the Last Minstrel* led William of Deloraine to the grave of Michael Scott. The outer side of this doorway is ornamented with an architrave of flowers and leaves so delicately chiselled that a straw can penetrate the interstices. Along the two remaining sides of the cloister, which originally formed a quadrangle, there are still some of the canopied sedilia, surmounted by a diaper frieze.

In the north transept there is a small-sized circular window, representing a crown of thorns ; and in the beautiful remaining fragment of the *North Aisle* may be seen a monumental stone erected in memory of the Kers (now Pringles) of Yair. The ruins are surrounded by an old churchyard, "where lie both great and small." On the south side of the nave Sir David Brewster is buried.

Leaving the Abbey and returning to the village, a fine view of the Tweed may be obtained from the Weir Hill, at the back of the parish church. A little below this the river is crossed by a chain bridge for foot-passengers, which conducts to the village of Gattonside.

The Eildon Hills (the *Tremontium* of the Romans, so called from their three summits) rise with an easy ascent immediately to the south of Melrose. The highest is 1385 feet above the level of the sea. They may be reached by the Dingleton road, which diverges from Melrose at the railway station. This hill-road crosses Bowden Moor to Bowden village and church, where the Dukes of Roxburghe have their family burial-place.

ABBOTSFORD,*

the residence of the late Sir Walter Scott, and now the property of James R. Hope Scott, Esq., Q.C., is situated three
miles to the west of Melrose, on the south side of the Tweed,
which at this place makes a beautiful sweep around the declivity. The entrance is by a porchway, adorned with petrified
stags' horns. The hall is panelled with richly-carved oak from
the palace of Dunfermline, and the roof consists of pointed
arches of the same material. Round the cornice there is a line
of richly blazoned coats-armorial, belonging to the principal old
border families. The floor is of black and white marble from
the Hebrides, and the walls are hung with ancient armour.
Adjoining the entrance-hall is the armoury, which runs quite
across the house, and communicates with the drawing-room on
the one side and the dining-room on the other.

The drawing-room is a lofty saloon, with wood of cedar. Its
antique ebony furniture, carved cabinets, etc., are all of beautiful workmanship.

The dining-room is a very handsome apartment, containing
a fine collection of pictures; the most interesting of which are
the head of Queen Mary in a charger, the day after she was beheaded, and full-length portraits of Lord Essex, Oliver Cromwell, Claverhouse, Charles II., and Charles XII. of Sweden; and
among several family pictures, one of Sir Walter's great-
grandfather, who allowed his beard to grow after the execution
of Charles I. The breakfast-parlour is a small apartment, overlooking the Tweed on the one side, and facing the hills of
Ettrick and Yarrow on the other. It contains a collection of
water-colour drawings, chiefly by Turner, and Thomson of
Duddingston, being the designs for the illustrated edition of
Scott's *Provincial Antiquities of Scotland.*

The library, the largest apartment, has an elegant roof of
carved oak, chiefly designed from models taken from Roslin

* Admission to Abbotsford House, 11 a.m. to 4 p.m. daily (except
Sunday), in February and March, thereafter on Tuesdays and Fridays.
Parties must not exceed ten at one time. Applications for larger excursion
parties to be addressed to Mr. Clabaux. This being a private residence
there is no stated gratuity, but the usual charge is 1s. for single visitors,
and 6d. each for parties of six.

Chapel. The collection of books amounts to many thousand volumes, many of them extremely rare and valuable. From the library there is a communication with the *Study*, where may be seen the small writing-table and plain arm-chair used by the great author. Round three sides there is a light gallery, which opens to a private staircase, by which he could descend from his bedroom unobserved. From this room we enter a small closet, containing the body-clothes worn by Sir Walter previous to his decease.

A little to the east of Abbotsford, below the junction of the Gala, is the vale of the Alwyn or Elwand Water, the supposed "Glendearg" of *The Monastery*.

Dryburgh Abbey.

This interesting abbey was founded about the year 1150, during the reign of David I., by Hugh de Moreville, Lord of Lauderdale, constable of Scotland. It is situated four miles to the east of Melrose, upon a richly wooded haugh, round which the Tweed makes a circuitous sweep. The site is supposed originally to have been a place of Druidical worship. Like Melrose, it consists of a church and an adjoining monastery. They are both built of the same stone, possessing the remarkable property of hardening with age. The architecture is of various periods, and displays both the Norman and Early English arch. The principal remains of the church are—the western gable of the nave, the chapter-house, and St. Moden's Chapel, the ends of the transept, and part of the choir and monastery. Opposite the door by which tourists are introduced* to the ruins is a yew-tree as old as the abbey. A double circle on the floor of the chapter-house marks the burial-place of the founder. St. Catherine's circular window, 12 feet in diameter, and much overgrown with ivy, is a beautiful feature in this part of the ruins. The nave of the church is 190 feet long by 75 broad, and under the high altar James Stuart (of the Darnley family), the last abbot, is buried. The refectory, or great dining-room of the monks, occupied the whole front of the abbey facing the

* The custodier lives at the entrance, where a visitors' book is kept. The charge for showing the ruins is 1s. for a party not exceeding three, and above that number at the rate of 4d. each.

south, and was 100 feet long by 30 feet broad, and 60 feet high.
Beneath it are the wine and almonry cellars.

St. Mary's Aisle, at once the most beautiful and interesting
part of the ruin, contains the burial-place of Sir Walter Scott,
who was interred here, 26th September 1832, in the tomb of his
maternal ancestors, the Haliburtons of Newmains, at one time
proprietors of the abbey. On either side are the tombs of his
wife and eldest son. His son-in-law, Mr. Lockhart, was also
buried in the same place in 1854. The same aisle is the place
of sepulture of the Erskines of Shieldfield and the Haigs of
Bemerside. In St. Moden's Chapel lie several members of the
Buchan family, ancestors of the present proprietors of the Dryburgh estate.

In the immediate vicinity of the abbey is the mansion-house
of Dryburgh, surrounded by stately trees. In a house within
the grounds once resided Ebenezer and Ralph Erskine, two
eminent Scottish divines, with whom originated the first
secession from the Established Church of Scotland. On a rocky
eminence overlooking the river is a rude colossal statue of the
patriot Wallace. A few miles down the Tweed is Mertoun
House, the seat of Lord Polwarth.

JEDBURGH,

[*Hotels:* Spread Eagle; Royal.]

the county town of Roxburghshire, lies to the S.E. of Melrose,
19 miles by rail, and 12 by the coach-road. It is a place of
antiquity, the old village of Jedworth having been founded by
Ecgred, Bishop of Lindisfarn, A.D. 845, and its castle is mentioned in the earliest Scottish annals. It was the chief town in
the Middle Marches.

The town has of late undergone great improvement; it has been
well drained, and supplied with excellent water, and the old
buildings pulled down to make way for new, and in many
instances elegant, structures, such as the Commercial Bank.

The Abbey, founded and endowed by David I. in 1118 or 1147
for Augustine friars from Beauvais, near Paris, occupies an
elevated position in the town, on the bank of the river Jed.

In common with other monasteries on the Border, it suffered
severely in the English invasions, and was for two hours exposed

to the artillery of the Earl of Surrey, who besieged Jedburgh in
the reign of Henry VIII. At the Reformation the abbey and
lands were converted into a temporal lordship in favour of Sir
Andrew Kerr of Ferniehirst, and they are now possessed by his
descendant, the Marquis of Lothian. In an architectural point
of view the building is interesting (like the neighbouring
Abbey of Kelso) for the mixed character of its arches and a
beautifully interlaced arcade. The principal entrance is by the
beautiful Norman door, which is ornamented with a profusion
of zig-zag mouldings, supported on slender shafts. The sides
of the gable are protected by two Norman buttresses, and the
summit is pierced by a St. Catherine's wheel, or rose window,
in the Flamboyant style. The clerestory consists of thirty-six
beautifully pointed windows. At the south-east extremity of
the nave is the burial-place of the late Lord Chancellor Campbell, who was a native of Jedburgh, and of his wife Lady Strath-
eden. The north transept, which is the only one remaining,
seems to have been rebuilt during the period of Middle
Pointed architecture, and is still entire. Above the great
north window are the arms of the Kerrs, the bailies of the
Abbey, whose burial-place is in this part of the church. The
oldest tombstone is dated 1524. The southern door, between the
central tower and Lord Campbell's vault, is a fine specimen of
Norman architecture.

The eastern extremity or apse is entirely destroyed, and the
site of the altar is occupied by a pretentious monumental tomb.
At this spot Alexander III. was married to Jolande, daughter
of the Count of Dreux (1285), in the presence of a brilliant
assemblage of French and Scottish nobility.

The small chapel adjoining the Norman door, on the south
side, was formerly the parish school, where Thomson, the author
of *The Seasons*, received part of his education. Here we are
under the great tower, 30 feet square and 120 high, rising
upon four circular arches, which may be ascended by a narrow
stair in the south-east corner. This tower commands a fine
view of the valley of the Jed, and the Cheviot Hills, which
divide Scotland from England.

In the neighbourhood of Jedburgh are *Ferniehirst Castle*, from
which the Marquis of Lothian takes his title as a British Peer ;
Ancrum House (Sir William Scott, Bart.) ; Mount Teviot

(Marquis of Lothian) ; Crailing, the seat of the Cranstouns ; and Bonjedward Bank (Major Pringle). Near this is the Roman causeway called Watling Street, which is still in a good state of preservation, and passes about two miles from the town.

From the top of the neighbouring hill called *The Dunion,* which is about 1031 feet high, there is a fine prospect of the whole valley of the Jed, and nearly the whole of Teviotdale, in the midst of which is situated the thriving manufacturing town of

HAWICK,

whose population (about 8000) are principally engaged in the manufacture of woollen cloth. About 2½ miles south-west of Hawick is Branksome Tower, the principal scene of Scott's *Lay of the Last Minstrel,* and once a residence of the Barons of Buccleuch.

In the same neighbourhood, eastwards, are Minto House, the seat of the Earl of Minto (the policies of which are open every day except Sunday), and the village of Denholm, where Leyden the poet was born.

KELSO.

[*Hotels:* The Cross Keys ; Queen's Head.]

This town occupies a beautiful situation on the margin of the Tweed, opposite its junction with the Teviot, 15 miles eastwards of Melrose, and 52 from Edinburgh.

The Abbey, standing alone, like some antique Titan predominating over the dwarfs of a later world, was begun in 1128— and so far completed as to receive the tomb of the founder's son, Earl Henry of Northumberland, in 1152. As a specimen of architecture it is partly Norman and partly Early Pointed. The form is that of a Greek cross, with the peculiar feature of having its head at the western extremity. A massive square tower rises over the axis, resting on four lofty centred arches, supported by tall piers of clustered columns. The entrance to the north transept is much admired. The abbey was reduced to its present ruinous state by the English, under the Earl of Hertford, in 1545, and the only parts remaining are the walls of the transepts, the centre tower and west end, and a small part of the choir. The lands and possessions of Kelso Abbey were conferred upon Sir Robert Ker of Cessford, by whose descendant, the Duke of Roxburghe, they are still enjoyed.

Floors, the seat of this nobleman, occupies a terraced lawn on the north bank of the Tweed, one mile westwards, and is one of the finest baronial edifices in Scotland. The Park is extensive and finely wooded. A holly marks the spot where James II. was killed by the bursting of a cannon at the siege of Roxburgh (A.D. 1460). Admission may be obtained to the grounds and gardens on Wednesdays, by application at the office of the National Bank of Scotland. The ruins of *Roxburghe Castle*, an early bulwark of the Border, are situated on the south side of the Tweed, on a neck of land between the Tweed and the Teviot.

The railway station is a quarter of a mile from the town, near which a turn of the road below Maxwellheugh affords one of the most picturesque views of Kelso, including the river Tweed, broadened into the dimensions almost of an estuary, and the bridge by which it is here crossed. On the south side appear the woods and mansion of Springwood (Sir George Douglas), while on the north side stands the town, with the ruins of the Abbey; the handsome modern residence of Ednam House (Mrs. Robertson); the elegant new Episcopal Chapel; the Free Church, with its conspicuous spire; the rich background of wooded heights, with Home Castle and the summits of the Eildons in the distance. The bridge is an elegant structure, consisting of five semi-elliptical arches, each 72 feet span, erected by Rennie, the architect of the Waterloo Bridge in London. The museum and library, situated on the Terrace, are open free on Mondays, Wednesdays, and Fridays, and well worthy of a visit.

There are numerous fine seats in the neighbourhood of Kelso.

At the mouth of the Tweed, on a gentle declivity, is situated the ancient burgh of

BERWICK-ON-TWEED,

[*Hotels:* King's Arms; Red Lion; Salmon. 58 miles from Edinburgh; 67 from Newcastle.]

which, having long maintained an independent position, was finally ceded to the English in 1482. Since then it has remained subject to the laws of England, though forming politically a distinct territory. The streets are spacious and well built, and the town is surrounded by walls, which only of late ceased to be regularly fortified. It is governed by a mayor, recorder, and justices ; and returns two members to Parliament. The trade of the port is not considerable. The castle, celebrated in early history, is now a shapeless ruin. The town is entered by five gates, called respectively the English, Scotch, Cow-port, etc. The railway bridge, which spans the Tweed from the Castlehill to the line on the Tweedmouth'side, presents a most graceful appearance from its great height and airy structure.

At Reston, 11 miles north-west of Berwick, a branch line strikes off to St. Boswells, where it joins the Waverley route. About midway on this branch is the quiet town of Dunse, supposed by some to have been the birthplace, in 1274, of the celebrated scholar Duns Scotus, whose *Quartum Librum Sententiarum* is one of the earliest specimens of black letter typography (1474). In the neighbourhood may be seen a remarkably fine specimen of an ancient British stronghold, called Edin's Hall, a supposed corruption of Odin's hauld.

Three miles to the north of Reston are the ruins of Coldingham Abbey, a remnant of early semi-Norman architecture. Near this, on the coast, is St. Abb's Head, a rugged promontory, on which there is a lighthouse. Perhaps no part of the British coast has afforded a richer treat to geologists than that lying between St. Abb's Head and Dunbar, over the whole of which Hutton and Playfair and Sir James Hall frequently wandered, and from which some of their favourite theories are derived. The coast is particularly striking at the promontory, deriving its name from Fast Castle, the "Wolf's Crag" of the *Bride of Lammermoor*, an ancient baronial fortress built upon the very point of the headland. The rocks here are the resort of numberless sea-fowl, and the dizzy heights are occasionally scaled in order to secure the eggs of the birds. Another of these geological phenomena is a remarkable ravine called the Peaths, a few miles westwards, over which the celebrated bridge of the same name was thrown in 1786. This singular structure is 123 feet in height, 300 feet in length, and 16 feet wide. The spot was aptly described in one of Oliver Cromwell's despatches as a place "where one man to hinder is better than twelve to make way."

STIRLING AND THE NORTH.

PROCEEDING from Edinburgh by this favourite route, the railway about eight miles westwards crosses the Almond Water by a fine viaduct, and there enters Linlithgowshire. To the right are seen the grounds of Newliston; and a short distance beyond a glance is obtained of the ruins of Niddry Castle, where Queen Mary passed her first night after her escape from Lochleven Castle. At the distance of 17 miles from Edinburgh, we reach the county town of

LINLITHGOW,

an old burgh, situated on the margin of a small lake, and famous for its old Palace, a favourite residence of the Stewart kings, and the birthplace of the unfortunate Queen Mary. It was in the adjoining church of St. Michael's that James IV. saw the apparition which warned him against his fatal expedition to Flodden Field; and from a house in the town, now removed, David Hamilton of Bothwellhaugh shot the Regent Moray as he was passing through. Linlithgow was of old celebrated for its wells; one of which, of elaborate form, stands in front of the town-house. The railway crosses the Avon valley by a viaduct, and enters Stirlingshire at Polmont Junction. Callander House, formerly the seat of the Earls of Linlithgow and Callander, is passed on the left; and in its vicinity may be seen portions of the interesting Roman antiquity called "Graham's Dyke," or wall of Antoninus. We next reach

FALKIRK,

a town of ancient origin, surrounded by extensive ironworks, and noted for its great cattle-markets or *trysts*. Proceeding onwards we reach Larbert, in the parish church of which, Bruce, the Abyssinian traveller, is interred. A few miles farther is Bannockburn, the scene of the famous battle fought at the beginning of the 14th century between Edward I. of England and Robert the Bruce of Scotland. Shortly after, we reach

STIRLING.

[*Hotels:* Golden Lion ; Royal ; Carmichael's Temperance.]

This ancient town is situated on a gradually sloping rocky ridge near the river Forth, and nearly equidistant from Edinburgh and Glasgow. Its castle, renowned in the history of the country, is placed on the brow of the ridge overlooking the Carse of Stirling, and is approached from the railway station by the main street, running up the back of the ridge to the esplanade. Here, on the south side, a beautiful new cemetery has been laid out, containing statues of Knox, Henderson, and other Reformers. Crossing the drawbridge, and passing below the Overport, we reach the upper square. Stopping here for a few minutes to admire the *Palace*, built by James V., of polished stone, relieved by grotesque figures and other ornamental work, we pass through a narrow passage at the side of the chapel royal (now used as a store-room and armoury), to an interesting building on the rampart, containing a room named after the Earl of Douglas, from a well-known incident in Scottish history.

The view from the battlements is beautiful and extensive, especially at a small opening in the parapet-wall termed "The Lady's Lookout," where we have spread out before us the vale of Menteith on the west, bounded by the Highland mountains. The view to the north and east comprehends the Ochil Hills and the windings of the Forth. The Campsie Hills close the southern prospect, and from the town, at our feet, the turnpike road guides the eye to the ruins of Cambuskenneth Abbey, the Wallace Monument, and Bridge of Allan.

Underneath the exterior wall, on the west of the castle, a road, called Ballangeich, furnished the fictitious name adopted by James V. in his various disguised adventures.

The castle is surrounded by a well-made walk, called the "*Back Walk*," which is so picturesque that it is well to follow it from its commencement. Parts of the old town-wall may

still be seen here, and also the Trades or Guild Hall, founded
by "Robert Spettall, taylor to King James IV." Near this is a
quaint building called COWANE'S HOSPITAL, surmounted by a
turret steeple. In the same vicinity stands the GREYFRIARS or
FRANCISCAN CHURCH (now called East and West Churches),
erected in 1494 by James IV., with some additions to the eastern
portion by Archbishop James Beaton, uncle of the cardinal.
This church is a fine specimen of the later pointed Gothic, and
a type of architecture peculiar to Scotland. Within its walls
the Earl of Arran, while regent of the kingdom, abjured
Romanism, and the coronation of the youthful James VI. took
place in the choir ; on which latter occasion John Knox
preached the coronation sermon. The massive Gothic columns
of the interior remain intact, and the external walls are in good
preservation. The transept was lately restored by Mr. Rochead
of Glasgow. Ebenezer Erskine, founder of the Secession Church
of Scotland, and whose mausoleum may be seen in front of the
church in St. John Street, was one of its ministers.

It was of old the fashion for the neighbouring nobles and
gentry to have their city mansions in provincial towns like
Stirling, and such was the distinguished use of many of the
buildings now devoted to humbler occupants. Argyle's Lodg-
ing (Broad Street), the most conspicuous of these mansions,
stands on the east side of the Castle Wynd, and is now used as
a military hospital. It belonged to the accomplished poet Sir
William Alexander, who in the reign of Charles I. was created
Earl of Stirling, and afterwards to the Argyle family, who
substituted their arms for those of the Alexanders. Here
Prince Charles, afterwards Charles II., enjoyed the hospitality
of the Marquis of Argyle, who little thought that his royal
guest was a few years later to send him to the scaffold. On
the opposite side of the street a new building occupies the site
of the house of the famous George Buchanan the historian. At
the head of Broad Street stand the ruins of a curious old building called MAR'S WORK, so named after the Earl of Mar, then
regent, who died before the building was completed. In the centre
are the royal arms of Scotland, and on the projecting towers, on
each side, those of the regent and his countess.

In the neighbourhood of Stirling there are some fine seats, including Polmaise Castle ; Powis, Boquhaun, Meiklewood, and

Leckie Houses; Gartier, Cardross, Craigforth, Kilbryde Castle, Larbert House, and Dunmore.

One of the most interesting antiquities in the neighbourhood of Stirling is Cambuskenneth Abbey, a fine specimen of the Early English or first pointed Gothic, though the tower, which is the only part remaining entire, is of a more heavy, massive, and Norman-looking character. On a spot near the high altar, pointed out by tradition as the burial-place of James III. and his Queen, an elegant modern tomb has been erected by her present Majesty.

The distance of Cambuskenneth from Stirling is only about a mile and a half by the ferry over the river Forth.

THE WALLACE MONUMENT.

The abbey before mentioned gives its name to the neighbouring cluster of rocks called the Abbey Craig, which rises to a height of 560 feet. The beauty of the situation and its vicinity to the scene of Wallace's first victory over the English, suggested it as a fitting site for the monument to the Scottish hero, which now crowns the cliff in the form of a lofty baronial tower. The monument, which was designed by Mr. Rochead of Glasgow, is 220 feet in height, and is surmounted by an open crown. It may be ascended by an open winding staircase; but those who do not relish the cork-screw process of ascent will be sufficiently rewarded by the view from the base.

STIRLING TO CASTLE CAMPBELL, RUMBLING BRIDGE, AND KINROSS, BY DEVON VALLEY RAILWAY.

This pleasant digressive tour introduces the stranger to the scenery of the Devon Valley and Ochil Hills, the nearest of which is Dunmyat. At a distance these mountains look like lofty mounds, as uniform as if they were artificially raised and smoothened, and destitute of breaks and variety of scenery. But they are in reality cut by deep clefts, so narrow as not to be visible at a distance.

At Alloa * we branch off northwards by the manufacturing villages

* ALLOA, the chief town of the county of Clackmannan, is a seaport, possessed of considerable trade and manufactures, and a hereditary fame for the brewing of good ale. Close by are the modern mansion of Alloa House (Earl of Kellie), and the remains of the ancient mansion of the Earls of Mar. The square tower of Clackmannan, which stands conspicuously on the summit of a hill two miles from Alloa, claims association with the great

of Tillicoultry and Alva, and at a distance of other 3 miles
reach the village of DOLLAR, noted for its academy, founded by
the late John Macnab.   In its vicinity is one of the most
picturesque ruins in Scotland—

CASTLE CAMPBELL,

an old fortress of the Argyll family, which occupies a peculiar
situation on the top of a high and almost insulated rock.   The
pathway by which it is approached commences about half-a-mile
to the northward of the village, and after describing the circuit of
.the glen terminates at the entrance of the rocky defile.

Part of the castle has an air of strength, but other portions are
light and decorated, and there is a noble hall with ribbed vaulting.
The castle suffered for its ownership in the great civil war, both on
account of the animosity of Montrose, and possibly also resent-
ment for the destruction of the "*bonnie House o' Airlie.*   It is now
the property of James Orr, Esq.

Four miles east of Dollar is the romantic spot called

THE RUMBLING BRIDGE,

where there is a good and comfortable hotel.

This scene takes its name from a small narrow arch, without a
parapet, which will be seen under the expanding arch of the new
bridge, as if it had been dropped into the cleft.   The ravine over
which it is thrown is covered with creeping plants and shrubs, kept
green by the spray of the stream which raves below, and farther
down makes the celebrated Falls of Devon.   The first but least
effective of these is "The Devil's Mill," which may be reached by
a footpath among the trees, commencing close to the inn.   Its
principal feature is a general hurry skurry of water among the
rocks, causing that thumping sound which is generally heard in a mill.

About a mile below this is *The Cauldron Linn*, a very striking
waterfall, and one of the finest in Scotland.   At two bounds the
river clears its way from the range of the Ochil chain into the
vale below.   Standing near the edge of the upper fall, we look
through a narrow opening in the rock into the valley below, where
the river is seen meandering calm and tranquil, as if it had madly
leaped no barriers, and no rocks impeded its course.   "The clear
winding Devon" has been celebrated by Burns in a beautiful lyric.

A short distance from the Rumbling Bridge is Aldie Castle, the
ancient seat of the Mercers of Aldie, now represented by Lady
Lansdowne, the youngest daughter of the late Baroness Keith.

King Robert Bruce. Farther east is Tulliallan Castle (Lady Villiers). The
distance by land from Alloa to Stirling Bridge is only six miles, while by
water it is twelve. A little to the westward of Alloa is Tullibody House,
the birthplace of the celebrated General Sir Ralph Abercromby.

KINROSS AND LOCHLEVEN CASTLE.

Those who are interested in the scenes connected with the unfortunate Queen Mary may be pleased to continue the journey from Rumbling Bridge to Kinross and Lochleven Castle, a distance of seven miles, occupying about twenty minutes.

At Kinross there is a good hotel (Kirkland's), and small boats may be hired for visiting the ruins of Lochleven Castle, which are situated on an island about half-a-mile from the shore. This castle is of great antiquity, but it derives its chief interest from having been the place of Queen Mary's imprisonment, the story of which is given, with all the embellishments of romance, by Sir Walter Scott in his novel of *The Abbot*.

When the Queen accomplished her escape the boat in which she sailed is said to have gone ashore on the lands of Coldon, at the south side of the lake, whence she was conducted by Lord Seton to Niddry Castle, near Linlithgow. The keys of the castle, which were thrown into the lake, were found many years afterwards, and presented to the Earl of Morton.

Lochleven is celebrated for its trout, and the right of fishing, with the use of a boat, may be obtained on application.

LAKE MENTEITH AND ABERFOYLE.

Another interesting excursion may be made from Stirling to Lake Menteith and Aberfoyle. Those desirous of only visiting the lake leave the railway at Port of Menteith station, 12¾ miles from Stirling. The station for those going direct to Aberfoyle is Bucklyvie, 15¼ miles from Stirling.

At Port of Menteith, 3½ miles from the railway station, there is a good hotel, where taking boat, the tourist will probably first land on the island of Talla, or "The Earl," containing the ruins of the feudal fortalice of the great Earls of Menteith.

The more interesting island is that called *Inch-mahome*, or the *Isle of Rest*, with its monastic ruins. This island is traditionally connected with the young Princess Mary, who was conveyed hither after the battle of Pinkie ; and a summer-house and hawthorn-tree are shown near the margin of the lake, as objects in which she took delight.

On leaving this lake we proceed on our way to Aberfoyle, 7 miles from the Bucklyvie station, and where there is a good hotel, "The Bailie Nicol Jarvie." At little more than a mile from the hotel, and close to the spot where the Duchray joins the Forth, stands the original Clachan. Here we reach the famous pass of Aberfoyle, now traversed by an excellent road.

This road is continued westwards along the margins of LOCHS ARD and CHON, to Stronachlachar, at the head of Loch Katrine.

STIRLING TO CALLANDER AND THE TROSSACHS, LOCH KATRINE,
AND LOCH LOMOND.

On leaving Stirling by this route we cross the Carse of Stirling,
through which meanders the river Forth, and obtain on one side
a fine view of the Highland mountains, and on the other of the
Wallace Monument and Abbey Craig. Shortly we reach the
Bridge of Allan, a favourite watering-place, occupying a fine sunny
situation on the side of a hill overlooking the vale of Stirling.
It contains two excellent hotels, a pump-room, and hydropathic
establishment, also numerous lodging-houses. The water for
which it is famous is of a saline nature. It flows cold from the
spring, but is generally drunk hot. The surrounding country is
beautiful, and there are numerous gentlemen's seats in the neighbourhood, including Westerton House (Col. Sir J. Alexander);
Airthrey Castle (Lord Abercromby); and Keir (the seat of the
Stirling-Maxwell family).

Passing a tunnel through the grounds of Kippenross, we reach
the old cathedral town of

DUNBLANE,

picturesquely situated on the banks of the river Allan. Its
Cathedral is one of the few fine specimens of Gothic architecture
in Scotland, and although wanting the elaborate decoration of
Melrose or Roslin, it excels both in beauty of proportion and
force of moulding. The western window, the beautiful little
window in the gable, and the arcading of the triforium, are
especially noteworthy. The tower is evidently the oldest part,
having decided marks of Norman work. Some of the prebends'
stalls and other pieces of carved work have been preserved, and
there are some interesting monuments.

One of the prelates of this see was the celebrated Archbishop
Leighton, who left his library to the clergy of the diocese. From
the back of the excellent hotel which is to be found here, the
tourist may enjoy a romantic walk on the banks of the river
Allan, and through the grounds of Kippenross (John Stirling,
Esq.), to the Bridge of Allan.

Passing from this to the river Teith, we enter more particularly on the *scenery of the "Lady of the Lake,"* commencing
fitly with the old village of DOUNE, where the Teith is spanned

TROSACHS & LOCH LOMOND.

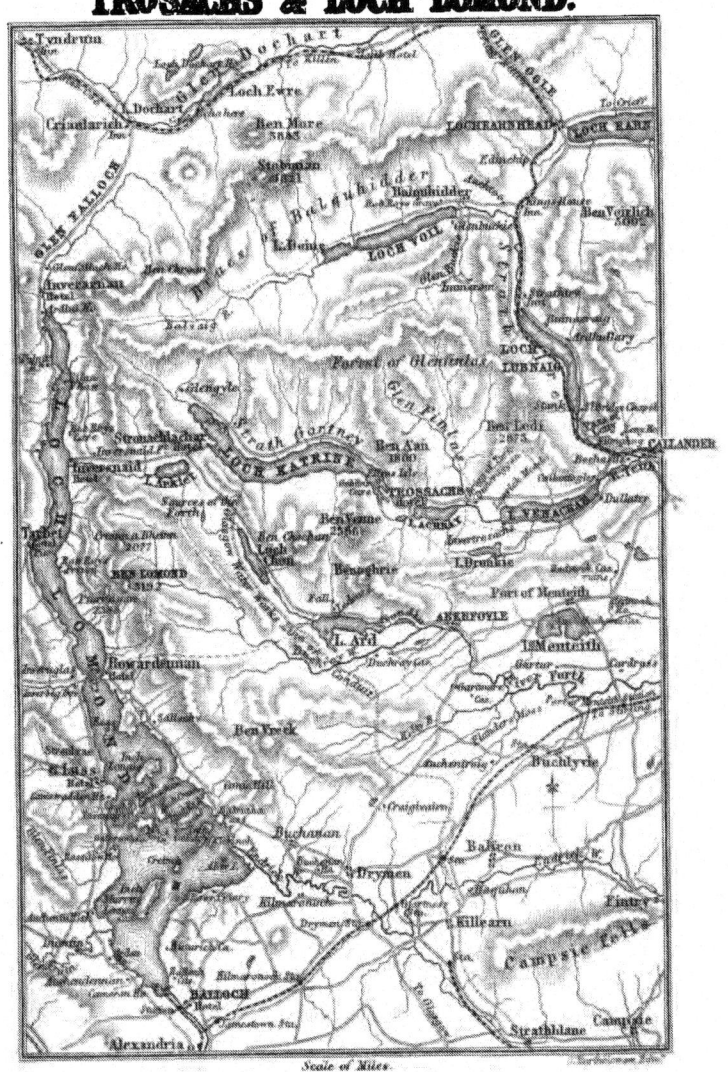

Scale of Miles

A. & C. Black, Edinburgh.

by a noble bridge—the work of Robert Spital, tailor to the queen of James IV. Above the bridge rise the towers of Murdoch of Albany's stronghold, roofless and ruinous, but still a majestic pile, with its two massive square towers, and high embattled walls. Most striking of all is its commanding site upon the steep banks of the river Teith.

About a mile to the north-west of Doune is Doune Lodge, a seat of the Earl of Moray. Proceeding along the northern bank of the Teith, the mountains Uam Var, Stuck-a-chroan, and Benvoirlich, are seen on the north, and on the opposite side we pass successively Lanrick Castle, Cambusmore (where Sir Walter Scott spent several summers), and the Gart. Just before arriving at Callander there may be seen, a little way *on the left* of the eastern station, a grassy embankment, covered with trees, supposed to be the remains of a Roman Camp. An excellent hotel (The Dreadnought) is close to the station, and M'Gregor's is not far distant.

CALLANDER

is a moderately-sized village, surrounded by several modern villas. To the tourist it forms a very convenient centre for excursions in this district.

An agreeable ramble of a few hours may be made to the Falls of Bracklinn, situated about two miles to the north-east of the village, and consisting of a series of shelving rapids and dark linns, formed by the river Kelty, which leaps from a considerable bank of red sandstone, among great masses of stone.

"There, gathering triple force, rapid and deep,
It boils, and wheels, and foams, and thunders through."

A longer excursion may be made by railway, through the Pass of Leny, to Loch Lubnaig, Lochearnhead, Balquhidder, and Killin. The line of railway is single, and of most picturesque construction. On leaving Callander it runs through the meadow land of Bochastle farm, where the waters from Lochs Venachar and Lubnaig unite and form the Teith. Here may be observed the ancient buryingground of the Buchanans. On the right is Leny Hous) (J. Buchanan Hamilton, Esq.) The line crosses the water, and passing under the road which leads to the Trossachs, runs close by the base of Benlêdi. It then skirts the side of the famous Pass of Leny, one of those ravines by which alone, in olden times, the Highlands were accessible from the south. The stream is twice crossed by means of substantial bridges, from either side of which beautiful peeps of scenery may be obtained. A little onwards are the church-

E

yard and ruins of St. Bride's Chapel, and half-a-mile beyond we
reach Loch Lubnaig, a fine sheet of water about five miles long and
one broad. The mountain side is so very steep and rugged, that great
difficulties were encountered in forming the railway, and at some places
arms of the loch had to be passed—not, as is often the case, by means
of bridges, but by embankments raised in the water.

After leaving Loch Lubnaig we pass along Strathyre, and cross
the Balvaig stream, at the distance of 9 miles from Callander.
Farther on, the foot of Glenbuckie is seen, and 2½ miles from
Strathyre village we pass King's House Inn, where, looking westwards, we obtain a view of the Braes of Balquhidder, and the old
church where Rob Roy is buried. The line passes Lochearnhead
at a distance of some 500 or 600 yards from the excellent hotel, and
as it is formed upon the slope of the hill at a great height, a
good view of Loch Earn is obtained, stretching to the east.

On leaving Lochearnhead we pass through a wild and desolate-
looking valley called Glen Ogle. The glen is narrow, and a
mountain stream, fed by numberless accessories, brawls along the
deep chasm. The railway is constructed upon the side of the
mountain, at the height of 300 or 400 feet above the level of the
valley, by means of several heavy cuttings and viaducts. One of
these has twelve arches of 35 feet in height, with a span throughout of 30 feet, and very strong foundations ; another viaduct is composed of three arches ; and several smaller viaducts of one arch have
been built for the purpose of allowing a passage to the mountain tor-
rents, which, in stormy weather, come down with great fury. Strong
retaining-walls have also been constructed ; and nothing has been
left undone which could add to the security of the line. At
Killin Station (4 miles from KILLIN village) the line turns westwards up Glen Dochart to TYNDRUM, and here enters a wild
country, eventually running down into Glenorchy by DALMALLY,
whence the line is being continued by Bonaw and Taynuilt to OBAN.
This is one of the most picturesque railway routes in the United
Kingdom.

Continuing the Trossachs route from Callander by one of the
coaches that runs on this much-frequented road, we proceed
westwards by Kilmahog toll, where, taking the turning to the
left, we cross the River Leny. The road beyond this winds
along a spur of Benledi, on the top of which lies "Samson's
Putting-stone," a large boulder, ready, apparently, to roll down
at the slightest touch. On the neighbouring height of Dunmore are the remains of an old British fort,

In the hollow to the south, near the ruins of an old mill, is
Coilantogle Ford, the spot where Roderick Dhu challenged
Fitz-James to single combat :—

> " See, here all vantageless I stand,
> Armed like thyself with single brand ;
> For this is Coilantogle Ford,
> And thou must keep thee with thy sword."

Shortly beyond this we reach Loch Venachar, a fine sheet of water, about five miles long, and a mile and a half broad. On the hillside at the west end of the loch may be seen Inver-trossachs shooting-lodge. In the hollow on the left of the road near this is Lanrick Mead, a flat meadow, which was the gathering ground of the Clan-Alpine. Half-a-mile farther we pass the Highland huts of Duncraggan, and the opening to the deer-forest of Glenfinlas, the property of the Earl of Moray. Close upon this is the bridge renowned from the simple couplet—

> " And when the Brigg of Turk was won,
> The headmost horseman rode alone."

Here we reach the margin of Loch Achray, where the scenery still preserves its gentle character—

> " The rocks—the bosky thickets sleep,
> So stilly in thy bosom deep ; "

Shortly after, the road makes a sudden bend, disclosing the spur of the mountain which forms the entrance to the Trossachs ; and a little beyond this, a slight deviation from the road at an old oak-tree brings us in front of the Trossachs Hotel, an elegant castellated building.

THE TROSSACHS extend from this to Loch Katrine, forming a wildering scene of mountains, rocks, and woods. Near the entrance of the gorge, the spot is pointed out where Fitz-James lost his " gallant grey."

At the distance of a mile or so from the Trossachs Hotel Loch Katrine comes in sight—

> " With promontory, creek, and bay,
> And mountains, that like giants stand,
> To sentinel enchanted land."

In a sheltered bay, at this end of the lake, a neat rustic pier has been erected for the accommodation of the steamer passengers.

Embarking here, we sail close by the island—

> " Where for retreat in dangerous hour
> Some chief had framed a rustic bower "—

and soon after obtain a complete view of Benvenue, which rises on the south to the height of 2386 feet, "throwing down upon the lake"

> "Crags, knolls, and mounds, confusedly hurl'd,
> The fragments of an earlier world."

The side of this mountain is broken by numerous corries and crags, which, softened by distance, are blended with the luxuriant herbage; and Coir-nan-Urisken, the *dread Goblin's Cave* of the "Lady of the Lake," seems but a gentle opening in the sloping ridge.

Near the west end of the loch is the commencement of the aqueduct by which the water of Loch Katrine is conveyed to Glasgow. Looking farther westwards from this point we see Glengyle, an old possession of the MacGregor family. At the west end of the lake is the pier of Stronachlachar, where passengers disembark and proceed by coach through Glen Arklet to Inversnaid on Loch Lomond, a distance of 5 miles; but, as the road is hilly, pedestrians, unencumbered with luggage, may as speedily walk the distance.

At Inversnaid a short time may be agreeably spent in visiting the waterfall formed by the river Arklet, and crossed by a slender foot-bridge, the scene of Wordsworth's "Highland Girl." A path leads up the water-side to a large boulder, from which there is a beautiful view of Loch Lomond.

At the pier of Inversnaid we meet the Loch Lomond steamer, and proceed either up or down the loch according to our arrangement of route.

LOCH LOMOND

is undoubtedly the finest of Scottish lakes. Its length is about 23 miles; breadth, where greatest, 5 miles, from which it gradually grows narrower, till it terminates in a prolonged stripe of water. The depth varies considerably; south of Luss it is rarely more than 20 fathoms; in the northern part it ranges from 60 to 100, and in the deepest places it never freezes. The steamer starts on its course from Balloch at the southern extremity of the loch, which is 20 miles from Glasgow, and 6 from Dumbarton. From thence it sails northwards, calling at the various piers on the shores, and threading its way among

"Those emerald isles, which calmly sleep
  On the blue bosom of the deep"—

the first and largest of the latter being Inch Murrin, which is
preserved as a deer-park by the Duke of Montrose.

On the eastern shore, opposite the islands, may be seen the
conical hill of Duncruin, Ross Priory (Sir George Leith), and
Buchanan House (the seat of the Duke of Montrose).

After touching at the pier of BALMAHA, the steamer crosses
to Luss, passing various islands, including Inchtavanach (Monks'
Isle), from which there is one of the finest views of the loch.

LUSS is a small village dependent on Sir James Colquhoun,
Bart., whose seat of Rossdhu is in the neighbourhood. Near
the village is Stronbrae, another fine point from which to obtain
a view of the loch.

From Luss northwards the breadth of the lake gradually con-
tracts, and the scenery becomes wilder. The steamer, recrossing
to the other shore, passes the wooded promontory of Ross to Row-
ARDENNAN, the usual starting-point for the ascent of Ben Lomond,
which rises immediately behind the hotel. This famous mountain
is 3192 feet in height, and the distance to the top is reckoned
four miles. There is a path by which ponies can reach the summit. The view which is here obtained is one of the finest in
Scotland, and comprehends the counties of Lanark, Renfrew, and
Ayr, the Firth of Clyde, Arran and Bute, to the south ; and the
counties of Stirling and the Lothians, with the windings of the
Forth, and the castles of Stirling and Edinburgh, to the east.

The steamer skirts the base of the mountain, where may be
seen an arch-shaped cavern, named Rob Roy's Prison.

"Yes, slender aid from fancy's glass
  It needs, as round these shores we pass,
  'Mid glen and thicket dark, to scan
  The wild MacGregor's savage clan."

We now reach TARBET, the landing-place for those who wish
to cross the isthmus to Arrochar and Loch Long, or to pursue
the coach-road through Glencroe, *via* "Rest-and-be-Thankful,"
to Inverary. The large and well-conducted hotel stands a short
way above the pier. Opposite is Inversnaid, where the passengers who have come thus far from the Trossachs, as already described, come on board, and about a mile above which is Rob
Roy's Cave.

The upper reach of Loch Lomond is narrow, and hemmed in by lofty mountains. Three miles from the head is Eilan Vow, containing the remains of a stronghold of the clan Macfarlane. At the head of the loch passengers disembark at a small pier, whence they are conveyed by omnibus to

INVERARNAN HOTEL,

a distance of 2 miles, situated at the entrance of Glenfalloch, in the midst of what may well be termed "mountain and flood." Tourists returning by the steamer have time to ramble about here for a few hours.

From this station there are several coach routes through the Highlands, in connection with the steamer, as follows :—

1. To Ballachulish through Glencoe ; 2. To Oban by Loch Awe ; 3. To Aberfeldy by Killin and Loch Tay.

The first of these routes (through Glencoe to Ballachulish) is 48 miles in length, and traverses some of the wildest scenery in Scotland. The road stretches northwards by Crianlarich and Tyndrum, across the dreary deer-forest of Blackmount, and past the boggy muir of Rannoch, to King's House Hotel. Three miles on the right is the steep ascent called the DEVIL'S STAIR-CASE, and here the tourist enters the famous GLENCOE.

After passing Invercoe House, the road for four miles skirts the banks of Loch Leven, a branch of Loch Linnhe, bounded by lofty mountains, and which, from its mouth to its farther extremity, is one succession of beautiful landscapes. Passing the slate-quarries, we reach

BALLACHULISH

with its fine new hotel, beautifully situated near the mouth of Loch Leven, and a few minutes' walk from the steamboat pier. This hotel forms a delightful halting-place, from which the tourist may proceed to Oban, or through the Caledonian Canal to Inverness.

The third route, alluded to above (viz., to Aberfeldy), diverges from the head of Glenfalloch at Crianlarich, and affords the tourist an opportunity of visiting the scenery of the district of Breadalbane, including Glen Dochart and Loch Tay, one of the most picturesque regions in Scotland.

PERTHSHIRE.

———◆———

OF all the counties of Scotland there is none so remarkable throughout for the beauty and variety of its scenery as Perthshire. Besides Perth proper, it comprehends the districts of Atholl, Breadalbane, Menteith, Strathearn, Stormont, Balquhidder, Gowrie, and Rannoch, all of which were formerly Stewartries, under the hereditary jurisdiction of the great proprietors, many of whose descendants still remain. It abounds with lakes and rivers, which occupy extensive valleys lying between lofty mountains. The principal town is

PERTH.

[*Hotels:* Royal George; Pople's British; Queen's; Salutation; Carmichael's. Temperance; Exchange.]

Perth is a city of great antiquity, to which tradition assigns a Roman foundation. It was often the residence of the Scottish monarchs, and has been the scene of some remarkable historical events. It was here that James I., one of the wisest and best of Scottish kings, fell a victim to the jealousy of his own aristocracy. Here also occurred the mysterious Gowrie conspiracy. The town itself is not particularly attractive, and there are no very fine buildings. The County Hall, facing the Tay, contains some full-length portraits by Sir T. Lawrence. At the north end of George Street is a stone building, erected in honour of Provost Marshall, containing a Public Library and Museum of Antiquities.

The principal church is *St. John's*, one of the few remaining collegiate churches of the middle-pointed age. The demolition of ecclesiastical architecture which accompanied the Reformation commenced in this church, in consequence of a sermon preached by John Knox against idolatry.

The river Tay is crossed at Perth by a handsome stone bridge of ten arches, from which a fine view is obtained. On either side are the meadows, called *The Inches*, about a mile and a half each in circumference. On the northern of these the famous combat between the Clan Chattan and the Clan Quhele (Kay) took place ; a subject which forms an interesting passage in Sir Walter Scott's "Fair Maid of Perth." Here a statue to the late Prince Consort has been erected. A statue of Scott faces the Tay at the foot of the High Street.

Perth is principally attractive in its environs, which include MONCREIFFE and KINNOULL HILLS, both of which are accessible by carriage roads. The fertile Carse of Gowrie,—the Firth of Tay, with the populous town of Dundee,—and the beautiful valley of Strathearn, are distinctly seen from these eminences. Pennant calls this view "the glory of Scotland." At the foot of Kinnoull Hill is Kinfauns Castle, surrounded by natural and artificial beauties.

About 5 miles south-west of Perth are Dupplin Castle, the seat of the Earl of Kinnoull, and the "Birks of Invermay," celebrated in song. SCONE PALACE, the seat of the Earl of Mansfield, who represents the old family of Stormont, is 2½ miles from Perth, on the left bank of the Tay. It is a large modern castellated building, and is built upon the site of the ancient palace of the kings of Scotland. On the removal from Dunstaffnage of the famous Stone of Destiny, on which the Scottish monarchs were crowned, it was deposited in the adjoining Abbey of Scone, until removed by Edward I. to Westminster, where it still forms part of the coronation-chair of the British monarchs. There is nothing left of Scone Abbey but an old aisle, now used as a mausoleum, and containing a marble monument to the memory of the first Viscount Stormont.

Those who are interested in round towers will find a very fine specimen at Abernethy, a village 8½ miles from Perth, supposed to have been an ancient Pictish capital. The tower is 74 feet in height, and built of square stones and with careful masonry.

A favourite district of Perthshire is that surrounding

CRIEFF,

a small town, agreeably situated on the river Earn, 17 miles from Perth by rail, and the same distance by road. It may also be reached by a branch from Crieff Junction on the Caledonian

Railway. It contains a good hotel, the Drummond Arms; and there is a well-conducted hydropathic establishment in the vicinity. As the centre of a picturesque Highland country it is almost unsurpassed, and to the health-seeker it has the advantage of a dry pure air. "If," says Mr. Bryant, the well known American poet, "there are any who desire to pass the entire summer without the uncomfortable sensation of being too warm, I can conscientiously recommend to them a sojourn in this beautiful region."

The environs include numerous rich and beautiful policies, and the proprietors exhibit the most praiseworthy liberality in the admission of strangers. Among these is DRUMMOND CASTLE, the original seat of the noble family of Perth, situated three miles to the south, and one mile from the village of Muthill. This castle is an ancient building, to which enlargements and improvements have been made from time to time. It is celebrated for its *gardens*, which are laid out in terraces in the Dutch style. Another beautiful seat in the neighbourhood of Crieff is OCHTERTYRE, the property of Sir Patrick Keith Murray, Bart. It is about two miles distant, and is approached by a fine avenue. Near the mansion there is a sheet of water, having on its banks a ruined fortress, erected in the 13th century by Comyn of Badenoch. The vale of the Turret exhibits a variety of romantic scenery, which has been rendered classical by the pen of Burns.

The other seats in the vicinity are Fern Tower (Lord Abercromby), Cultoquhey, Inchbrakie, Tulchan, Abercairney (Home Drummond Moray, Esq.), and Monzie Castle. The castle and collegiate church of Innerpeffray stand about three miles southeastwards, and six miles westwards is the village of COMRIE, which has acquired a notoriety from being subject to earthquakes. From Comrie the tourist may visit Loch Earn, and at Lochearnhead join the railway from Callander to Killin.

An excursion often made from Crieff conducts the tourist to the Small Glen and Glen Almond, by Foulford Inn and Amulree. This is the spot alluded to by Wordsworth in his beautiful stanza:—

"In this still place, remote from men,
Sleeps Ossian in the narrow glen "—

in reference to the tradition that a large stone in the valley covers the remains of the Scottish bard.

Returning to Perth, and proceeding northwards by railway, we reach, at a distance of about 16 miles, the town of

DUNKELD,

where there are some excellent hotels, including the Birnam, at the station ; Athole Arms, close to the bridge ; and Royal, at the entrance to the Ducal grounds, and very comfortable.

The village of Birnam, consisting of a few houses, shops, and villas, in the vicinity of the railway station, forms a modern suburb to Dunkeld. In front of the hotel Birnam Hill rises to the height of 1580 feet, and a well-made road of three miles in length reaches nearly to the summit. Extensive views are obtained from this hill ; but a more diversified prospect is got from the lower elevation of Craig-y-barns on the other side of the Tay.

The village of Dunkeld itself is narrow and ill-built, but there are few places of which the first sight is so striking. This is owing to its noble river, crossed by a fine bridge, and its cathedral nestling among wooded mountains. The Duke of Athole has a residence here, and the principal objects of attraction are contained within his grounds, to which strangers are admitted on payment of a small fee to the guide. In proceeding through these we reach first the Cathedral, the choir of which is still used as the parish church. It is believed that the origin of this cathedral was a religious cell, established by the disciples of St. Columba (Culdees), and that Kenneth Macalpin, anxious to testify his respect for the relics of this apostle of the Scots, removed them hither from Iona. The architecture is of a composite character, exhibiting features both of the Norman and Pointed styles. Perhaps its most characteristic feature is the *Tower*, which is about 90 feet high, and stands at the west end of the north aisle.

Of the monuments that have survived the general destruction, the most remarkable is a recumbent figure in armour of the notorious Wolf of Badenoch. The most celebrated Bishop of Dunkeld was Gawain Douglas, who

"In a barbarous age
Gave to rude Scotland Virgil's page."

Near the Cathedral are two of the earliest larches introduced into Britain from the Tyrol, in 1738.

From the Cathedral it is usual to conduct strangers to what forms a most attractive scene—namely, the cataract of the river Braan, situated where the so-called Ossian's Hall or Hermitage formerly stood. About a mile higher up the same stream is a fine waterfall, which precipitates itself down a narrow and deep chasm, crossed by a bridge, hence called the *Rumbling Bridge*, 80 feet above the waterway. Into this gulph the river pours itself with great fury, foaming and roaring over massive fragments of rock, and casting up a thick cloud of spray. In picturesque features this fall is inferior to the other, but both depend much on the state of the weather.

On the way homewards we pass the hamlet of Inver, where Neil Gow, the well-known violinist and composer of Scotch reel-tunes, resided.

A beautiful walk may be taken from Birnam by the banks of Tay, to MURTHLY CASTLE, a modern mansion, erected from a design by the late Mr. Gillespie Graham of Edinburgh, in the Elizabethan style, but left incomplete. There are numerous other seats in the neighbourhood, including Eastwood House, St. Mary's Tower, Rochallion, Kinloch, Meikleour, Erigmore, Glendelvine, and others.

Excursions may be made from Dunkeld to Blairgowrie by Cluny, a distance of 12 miles—a route comprising scenery of a pleasing though not romantic nature; and to Pitlochrie by Logierait and Moulinearn, a distance of 13 miles.

Detour from Dunkeld or Ballinluig Station.

ABERFELDY—KENMORE AND LOCH TAY.

Before leaving this district it is necessary to notice the beautiful scenery in the neighbourhood of Loch Tay, which may be readily visited from Dunkeld, proceeding from thence by rail as far as Aberfeldy, and thence by coach. There is an excellent hotel at Aberfeldy, "The Breadalbane Arms," immediately opposite which is the entrance to the FALLS OF MONESS, described by Burns—

> " The braes ascend like lofty wa's,
> The foaming stream, deep roaring, fa's,
> O'erhung wi' fragrant spreading shaws,
> The Birks of Aberfeldy.

The Tay is crossed here by one of General Wade's bridges, where the companies of the Black Watch were embodied into the 42d regiment. About a mile distant by this bridge is the Weem Hotel, a delightful station for the tourist.

A coach, running in connection with the railway, conveys tourists onwards to the village of

KENMORE,

a distance of 6 miles. Here there is an excellent hotel, the Breadalbane Arms, situated close to the principal entrance to Taymouth Castle, the seat of the Earl of Breadalbane.

This splendid mansion stands on an extensive lawn, at the base of Drummond Hill, within a mile of the village. As a building it is somewhat sombre in aspect, but this is redeemed by the pleasure-grounds with which it is surrounded, and which possess a striking combination of beauty and grandeur. As Burns wrote in the inn parlour during his short sojourn :—

> "Here poesy might wake her heaven-taught lyre,
> And look through nature with creative fire."

An excursion may be made from Kenmore to the Falls of Acharn, a cascade 2 miles distant, on the south side of Loch Tay. The fall is about 80 feet high, and an excellent view of it is obtained from the "hermit's mossy cell."

Of Loch Tay, which is here viewed with better effect than elsewhere, it is difficult to speak but in the most glowing terms, as again remarks Burns :—

> "The outstretching lake, embosom'd 'mong the hills,
> The eye with wonder and amazement fills."

It is one of those long narrow lochs which occur frequently in Scotland, extending 15 miles from east to west, and being little more than about one mile in breadth at any part. At its south-western extremity, near Killin, it receives the united streams of the Dochart and Lochy, and discharges its waters at the north-east end, at Kenmore, by the river Tay. Its depth varies from 15 to 100 fathoms. The banks on both sides are finely diversified by the windings of the coast and the imposing aspect of the surrounding mountains. It contains only one very small island, which lies off the coast near Kenmore. On this island may still be seen the ruins of a priory founded by Alexander I., who deposited within it the remains of his Queen

Sybilla, daughter of Henry I. of England. The loch abounds with salmon and trout, and the exclusive right of fishing belongs to the Earl of Breadalbane.

The distance from Kenmore to Killin is 16 miles, and the road follows the northern shore of Loch Tay. About midway is BEN LAWERS, one of the highest mountains in Scotland (3984), and the loftiest in the county of Perth. At Killin we regain the railway connecting Dalmally and Oban with Callander. (See p. 50.)

Killin is a fine specimen of an old Highland village, and formerly was the seat of the Clan M'Nab, whose burial-place is situated on an island amid the rushing waters of the Dochart. Near the Free Church of the village a grave is pointed out as that of Fingal's, and within a short distance are the ruins of Finlarig Castle, and the mausoleum of the Breadalbane family, surrounded by some fine old trees.

The Highland Railway.

The county of Perth is intersected from north to south by the Highland Railway, which is carried along the banks of the Tay, through the famous Pass of Killiecrankie, and thence through Glengarry, after which it crosses an angle of Inverness-shire into Nairnshire. The whole distance from Perth to Inverness is 144 miles. The route affords a rapid means of viewing some of the most noted Highland scenery, and it is also the most direct between the north and south of Scotland. Having already described Perth and Dunkeld, we continue the journey from the latter.

At BALLINLUIG Station we reach the junction for Aberfeldy, near which the Tay is joined by the Tummel. On the summit of the promontory which separates these rivers stands a monument to the late Duke of Athole. The next station is PITLOCHRIE, with its excellent hotel (Fisher's). This village is agreeably situated in a healthy part of the country, in consequence of which a large Hydropathic Establishment and numerous villas have been erected in its neighbourhood. It is the key to several scenes of interest, including Lochs Tummel and Rannoch.

About a mile east of the village is Spout-dhu, a waterfall, nearly 100 feet in height, formed by the Edradour Burn. Ben Vracky, one of the Grampians, the summit of which is 2800 feet high, is about 3 miles to the north, and may easily be ascended in two hours. The loch and falls of Tummel form an easy and agreeable excursion.

About 2 miles beyond Pitlochrie we pass Faskally House (Archibald Butter, Esq.), and soon after the railway proceeds through the historically famous pass of

KILLIECRANKIE

by a viaduct of ten arches, 54 feet high and 36 feet span. A little beyond the north end of the pass is the scene of the battle, fought in 1689, between the Highland clans under Viscount Dundee, and the troops of King William III.; and a stone in the park fronting Urrard House marks the spot where Dundee received his death-wound. We next reach

BLAIR-ATHOLE,

a Highland hamlet with a good hotel (The Athole Arms), and noted for the wild scenery amid which it is situated. The particular objects of attraction here are the falls of the Fender and Bruar. The former are formed by a streamlet, which descends Ben-y-Gloe, through a deep ravine, and discharges its waters into the Tilt.

The Falls of the Bruar, situated three miles to the westward, form a charming scene well worthy of a visit. The stream makes two distinct sets of falls, rushing, in the lower, through a perpendicular channel. It is interesting to know that the fir plantation on the sloping banks above was planted by the Duke of Athole, in deference to Burns' "Petition." And now

> "Lofty firs and ashes cool,
> The lowly banks o'erspread,
> And view, deep-bending in the pool,
> Their shadows' watery bed."

The upper fall is divided into three parts, the aggregate height of which is estimated at 200 feet. A carriage-road leads as far as the second set of falls, and numerous walks have been cut through the plantation.

Blair Castle, the ancient residence of the Earls of Athole, is situated about half-a-mile to the north of the village. It consists of a range of castellated buildings, and was once the property of the great family of Comyn.

A stone-cast above is the old church of Blair, where Viscount Dundee was buried after the battle of Killiecrankie.

The valley of Glen Tilt branches off at Blair-Athole into the mountain-ranges of Ben-y-Gloe, and the lofty hills that form the northern part of the Athole forest. This enormous tract of wild mountain extends over nearly 100,000 English acres, and is estimated to contain about 10,000 head of deer. There is a mountain path through the glen to Braemar, a distance of 30 miles.

From the diversified scenery which is to be found about Blair-Athole the railway passes on into a bare and inhospitable country, very thinly populated. Little falls to be observed except the bleak and by no means varied character of the surrounding hills, which form the great forest of Drumouchter, until the upper end of Loch Garry appears, a welcome and interesting object on the left, near the lovely shooting-lodge and station of DALNASPIDAL. Near this the counties of Perth and Inverness join. After passing the well-known mountains, called the "Badenoch Boar" and "Athole Sow," on the left, and the upper end of Loch Ericht, we reach DALWHINNIE, where the roads to Inverness, Fort-Augustus, and Fort-William meet. Here the railway enters Badenoch, an immense tract of Highland territory, from which the ancient family of Comyn were designed ; thence passing through Glentruim, the Spey is reached, and crossed by an eight-spanned bridge of nearly 300 feet in length. We soon thereafter arrive at

KINGUSSIE,

the station for those who wish to proceed to Fort-William by coach, and where there is an excellent hotel. On the other side of the Spey are the ruins of Ruthven Barracks, formerly one of the principal residences of the Comyns.

On leaving Kingussie, the landscape becomes much more interesting, and the extensive embankments of the Spey and the meadows of Belleville House appear to great advantage, until the river falls into the Loch of Insh. On the left is the village of Lynchatt (Cat's linn) ; north of which stands a small monument to Macpherson of Belleville, the translator of Ossian. On the right is the House of Milton, close by the village of Insh ; and to the south are Glens Tromie and Fishie, near the latter of which is the cottage-looking house of Invereshie (Sir George M. Grant, Bart.) On the left, near BOAT OF INSH, is Kincraig House (Mackintosh of Mackintosh). After this there is a succession of mountain-scenery. The pretty loch and parish church of Alvie are seen on the left, and the Tor of Alvie upon the right. On the top there is a cairn to the memory of the Highlanders who fell at Waterloo, and a monument to the last Duke of Gordon. On passing Tor Alvie, the Doune of Rothiemurchus (J. P. Grant, Esq.), and the immense pine-forests of Rothiemurchus and Glenmore, with the Cairngorm and lower Grampian ranges, are seen on the right ; on the left is the rugged birch-clad mountain of Craigellachie (the Rock of Alarm), the rendezvous in former times of the clan Grant. At AVIEMORE the tourist is within four miles of the celebrated castle of Loch-an-eillan, and at BOAT OF GARTEN a line of railway branches off through Strathspey, by Abernethy and Rothes, to Elgin. To the right of the line is the large farm-house of Tullochgorum, which has been rendered famous by Skinner's well-known song ; and farther on are the village and bridge of Nethy, and the ruins of Castle Roy. Before coming to the romantic stream of Dulnain, we obtain a glimpse of Strathspey, and of the peaked hill of Benrinnes, which rises over the ancient house of Ballindalloch. After crossing the Water of Allan the train reaches GRANTOWN, the capital of Strathspey, where there is a good hotel (The Grant Arms). In its vicinity is Castle Grant, a seat of the Earl of Seafield, in which there are some interesting paintings. Beyond Grantown the railway enters Brae Moray, a wild district of country. A few miles to the west of DAVA Station lies the desolate Loch-an-Dorb, with the ruins of an extensive castle, which figured as a royal fortress in the early history of Scotland, and afterwards as a possession of the Earls of Moray and Campbells of Cawdor. Crossing the Divie by means of a magnificent viaduct, below which the manse, church, and burial-ground of Edinkillie are picturesquely situated, we next reach DUNPHAIL, in the neighbourhood of which is Dunphail House (Major Cumming Bruce). A district succeeds, studded with gentlemen's seats ; and at times views are obtained of the Moray Firth, the Sutors of Cromarty, and the northern mountains. The village of Rafford and the old white-washed town of Blervie are seen to the right ; and on the left is Sanquhar House

(C. Fraser Tytler, Esq.), with its beautiful grounds and parks. We now arrive at the thriving town of FORRES, where the junction is made with the line from Aberdeen *via* Keith, by which we proceed to INVERNESS. This town is described in a subsequent page, in connection with the Caledonian Canal route (page 124).

THE NORTH-EASTERN DISTRICT OF SCOTLAND.

DUNDEE—ST. ANDREWS—FORFAR—ARBROATH—BRECHIN —MONTROSE—STONEHAVEN—ABERDEEN—DEESIDE AND BRAEMAR.

DUNDEE.

[*Hotels:* Royal; British; Crown; Dundee Arms; Lamb's Temperance.]

This large city is the third in Scotland in extent of population, and the principal seat of the linen trade of the United Kingdom. It is situated in Forfarshire, on the north bank and near the mouth of the river Tay, 22 miles from Perth and 50 from Edinburgh. It bears considerable resemblance to a continental town—that is, the houses are old, lofty, and dark, and many of the streets gloomy. In a maritime and manufacturing point of view, it is a place of great importance, its splendid docks testifying to the former, as its elegantly built and extensive manufactories do to the latter. Connected with the docks, spacious quays and tide-harbours extend along the margin of the Tay for a mile and a half. Here are Customs and Excise Offices; and the Royal Arch, built in commemoration of the Queen's visit in 1844, which is one of the chief ornamental structures of the town. The harbour works are faced by an elegant *Esplanade*, which has been constructed with the view of deepening the river by increasing the force of the current.

The market-place or High Street consists of a spacious square, from which diverge the Overgate, Nethergate, Seagate, and Murraygate, which run west and east, nearly parallel with the river. Castle Street leads from the south-east end of the High Street to the docks on the south, and contains the theatre, and at its lower extremity the handsome Exchange Rooms. On the south

F

side of the market-place stands the Town House. In a crescent at the head of Reform Street is the High School, and near it stands the Post-office.

In West Bell Street, adjoining the prison, is the Sheriff Court-house. In this vicinity is situated the Volunteer Drill Hall, which contains a Gymnasium. The Royal Exchange is situated in Panmure Street, and opposite to it is the office of the Union Bank of Scotland, etc. The Episcopal Church of St. Paul's is a fine building of the decorated Gothic order, designed by Sir G. Scott, occupying the site of the old castle of Dundee. The *Albert Institute*, erected in honour of the late Prince Consort, contains on the upper floor a lecture-hall, and on the lower the *Free Library*, being the first of its kind established in any of the large towns of Scotland. The surrounding open space, called Albert Square, contains a large ornamental fountain, designed also by Sir G. Scott, and a statue of the late George Kinloch, Esq., first M.P. for the burgh in the reformed parliament of 1832.

On the north side of the Nethergate is the remarkable square tower or *old Steeple of St. Mary's Church*, one of the greatest architectural curiosities in Scotland. It is 156 feet in height, and is said by Hector Boece, the historian (who was born at Dundee), to have been founded by David, Earl of Huntingdon, brother of the Scottish monarch William I., in gratitude for his deliverance from shipwreck in the Tay. But it is held by others to be of earlier date. The old church was destroyed by fire in 1841, and has been replaced by two modern churches.

The Barracks of Dundee (occupying the site of *Dudhope Castle*, the seat of the ancient Constables of Dundee) consist of a terrace on the lower slope of the Law, about half-a-mile from the High Street. A little to the eastward is *The Royal Infirmary*, the largest and most conspicuous of the public buildings of Dundee. From this we may ascend to the top of *The Law*, the round green hill in the rear of the town. It is 535 feet in height, and commands an extensive panoramic view, including the mouth of the Tay, the Bell Rock Lighthouse, the bay and town of St. Andrews, and the German Ocean. At the north-eastern extremity of the town lies *The Baxter Park*, which was presented by Sir David Baxter, Bart., of Kilmaron, and his two sisters, to the town. It is 38 acres in extent, commands an extensive view

of the river Tay and surrounding country, and was laid out in
a very tasteful manner by the late Sir Joseph Paxton. About a
quarter of a mile east of this is *The Eastern Necropolis*, containing a number of handsome monuments.

On ground to the north-west of the Baxter Park is *The Mor-
gan Hospital*, an institution, modelled after Heriot's in Edinburgh, for the education of sons of decayed tradesmen. The
principal manufactures of Dundee are fabrics of linen, hemp,
and jute.

Of late years great improvements have been made in the spin-
ning-mills, some of which are quite palatial in extent and appearance.

St. Andrews.

[*Hotels:* The Royal; Cross Keys.]

This ancient episcopal city is situated in a fine bay on the extreme east coast of Fifeshire. It may be conveniently reached
from Dundee, from which it is 16 miles distant (occupying
about an hour by railway), while from Perth it is 37, and from
Edinburgh 45 miles distant. Its origin is attributed to St.
Regulus, who was shipwrecked here about the end of the 4th
century, and the ruins of a chapel and an entire tower, known
by this name, are still to be seen near the Cathedral.

The Cathedral was founded in the year 1159 by Bishop
Arnold, and completed by Bishop Lamberton in 1318. Its
original length was 350 feet, the breadth 65, and the transept 188
feet; but nearly the whole of the fabric was pulled down by an
infuriated mob, excited by a sermon preached by John Knox
against idolatry, in the parish church of St. Andrews. The
solitary remnants consist of the eastern gable, half of the western,
part of the south side wall and of the transept. The prior of St.
Andrews had precedence of all abbots and priors, and on festival
days had a right to wear a mitre and all episcopal ornaments.

The remains of the *Castle* of St. Andrews stand upon a rock
overlooking the sea, on the north-east side of the city. This
fortress was founded, about the year 1200, by Roger, one of the
bishops, and repaired towards the end of the 14th century by
Bishop Trail. It was the birthplace of James III., and obtained
subsequently a memorable notoriety as the scene of the cruel burn-
ing of Wishart the reformer. This event took place in front of the

apartment occupied by Cardinal Beaton, who was himself surprised in turn, and assassinated by Norman Lesley. The castle was at that time almost demolished, and its picturesque ruins have since served as a landmark to mariners.

THE UNIVERSITY of St. Andrews—the oldest in Scotland—was founded in 1411 by Bishop Wardlaw. It consisted originally of three colleges—St. Salvator's, St. Leonard's, and St. Mary's; the first two being now united. *St. Salvator's* was founded by Bishop Kennedy in 1458, and formed originally an extensive building with a quadrangle, and a gateway surmounted by a spire. That having fallen into decay, the present Hall was erected for the better accommodation of the students. Before the old gateway it is interesting to know that the celebrated martyr Patrick Hamilton was burned. *St. Leonard's* was founded by Prior Hepburn in 1532, and the buildings, which include the study of the celebrated George Buchanan, are used as a private dwelling. *New* or *St. Mary's College* was established by Bishop Hamilton in 1552: it stands in a different part of the town, and is reserved exclusively for theology.

The Madras College of St. Andrews is an admirable school, established in the year 1833 by the late Dr. Andrew Bell, a native of the town, and inventor of the monitorial system, who bestowed the munificent sum of £60,000 upon its foundation. The buildings, which are elegant, stand on the site of the Blackfriars Monastery, the fine old chapel of which still remains. The fees being low, and in many cases not exacted, the school has been very successful.

The Parish Church, a spacious structure, contains a lofty monument of white marble in honour of Archbishop Sharp, who was murdered by some of the exasperated Covenanters, in revenge for his oppressive conduct. *The College Church*, which belongs to the United College, is situated to the north of this. It was founded in 1458 by Bishop Kennedy, and contains a beautiful tomb, erected to his memory, of exquisite Gothic workmanship, though much injured by time. About the year 1683, six highly ornamented silver maces were discovered within it, which had been concealed there in times of trouble. Along with these interesting relics are shown John Knox's pulpit, and some silver arrows, inscribed with the arms and names of victors in the annual competitions.

At the west end of the town one of the original massive portals is preserved unimpaired. The city has about it an air of seclusion, and contains some curious antique houses, which were once occupied by persons of rank.

The Links of St. Andrews constitute one of its main attractions, affording, as they do, one of the finest fields for the game of golf. The golf-club house is a neat building on the links.

FALKLAND PALACE (FIFE).

Those who are interested in ancient Scottish buildings may be reminded while here of the old palace of Falkland, which occupies a central position in the same county, being 3 miles from Falkland Road station on the Fife line of railway, and 27 from Edinburgh. The building, interesting alike in a historical and architectural point of view, is situated in the village of Falkland, where there is a good inn—The Bruce Arms. The building is kept in good condition, and part of it forms a very handsome dwelling-house. The surrounding grounds are also kept in the best order by the proprietrix, Mrs. Tyndal Bruce, whose beautiful residence of Nuthill is a little to the westwards. "The western front," says Mr. Billings, "has two round towers, which are a diminutive imitation of those at Holyrood, and stretching southwards is a range of building, with niches and statues, which perhaps bears as close a resemblance to the depressed or perpendicular style of the English semi-ecclesiastical architecture as any other building existing in Scotland." The east side, again, is diversified by renovations of classical architecture. The parts wanting to complete the quadrangle were destroyed by fire in the reign of Charles II. No portion of the present edifice appears to be of great antiquity. A painful interest attaches to its walls from its having been the place of imprisonment of David, Duke of Rothesay, eldest son of Robert III., who suffered here the agonies of death by starvation. The tragedy is heightened by the tradition that the life of the unfortunate prisoner was sustained for a time by a woman's milk, conveyed from her breast through a reed; an incident interwoven with Scott's novel of the "Fair Maid of Perth."

About 6 miles to the north of St. Andrews there is an interesting remnant of church architecture, viz. the chancel and

apse of Leuchars church, said to be the best specimen of
Norman architecture in Scotland. A few miles from Cupar, the
county town of Fife, there is a spot interesting to geologists,
called the Den of Durie.

Returning to the district of Dundee, we proceed to

FORFAR,

the county town, situated in the interior, 14 miles to the
north of that city. It is a place of great antiquity, having
been a royal residence in the time of Malcolm Canmore, and
anciently contained two castles. In the county hall is preserved a curious instrument of torture called "the witches'
bridle," which was placed over the heads of the miserable
creatures burnt for witchcraft. On the walls are hung portraits
of Admiral Duncan and others, by Opie, Raeburn, etc. The
trade of Forfar is of the same nature as that of Dundee.

About six miles to the west of Forfar is the celebrated castle of

GLAMIS,

the hereditary seat of the Earls of Strathmore and Kinghorn, and
interesting both on account of its historical associations and
the elaborate style of its architecture. It is shown on Fridays
only. The *Garden* is of great extent, and laid out with much
taste.

"I was only 19 or 20 years old," says Sir Walter Scott,
"when I happened to pass a night in this magnificent old
baronial castle. The hoary old pile contains much in its
appearance, and in the traditions connected with it, impressive
to the imagination. It was the scene of the murder of a Scottish king of great antiquity; not indeed the gracious Duncan,
with whom the name naturally associates it, but Malcolm II.
It contains also a curious monument of the peril of feudal times,
being a secret chamber, the entrance of which, by the law or
custom of the family, must only be known to three persons at
once—viz. the Earl of Strathmore, his heir-apparent, and any
third person whom they may take into their confidence."

ARBROATH,

another seaport and manufacturing town of Forfarshire, stands next to Dundee in point of trade and population, but possesses little to attract the tourist except its fine old Abbey, founded by William the Lion in 1178, and dedicated to the English martyr, Thomas à Becket. The founder was interred within its precincts, and a grave composed of hewn freestone, near the site of the high altar, is supposed to contain his remains. The last abbot was the famous Cardinal Beaton, who was at the same time Archbishop of St. Andrews. The ruins are greatly dilapidated, and chiefly interesting in their details. The chancel has evidently been the noblest part of the building, and the eastern window is still entire.

Twelve miles off the coast of Arbroath stands the Bell-rock or Inch-cape Lighthouse. Formerly the Abbot of Aberbrothock had a floating bell moored on this rock, whose warning toll was heard during a storm. According to a tradition, which forms the subject of one of Southey's popular ballads, the bell was on one occasion wantonly cut away by a pirate, whose vessel afterwards, by a strange retribution, drifted on the rock and perished with her crew.

In the neighbourhood of Arbroath are — Letham Grange (—— Miln, Esq.), Kinblethmont (Lindsay Carnegie, Esq.), and Eathie (Earl of Northesk).

The next town of importance in Forfarshire is

BRECHIN,

situated on the banks of the South Esk, 14 miles to the north of Arbroath, and 7½ west from Montrose. It carries on a considerable manufacture of linen, and there are extensive freestone quarries in the neighbourhood. In ancient times Brechin contained an abbey of Culdees, and a bishopric was subsequently established here by David I. There was also a cathedral, which occupied a romantic situation near the edge of a ravine, but it was almost wholly destroyed in repairing it as a modern place of worship. Adjoining the church is a *round tower* of the same type as that of Abernethy. *Brechin Castle*, a seat of the Maule

family, now represented by the Earl of Dalhousie, stands on a
precipitous rock ; and the chief seats in the neighbourhood are
Auldbar Castle (P. Chalmers, Esq.) and Kinnaird Castle (Earl of
Southesk), both beautifully situated amid forests and ornamental
plantations.

An excursion frequently made from Brechin conducts the
tourist to Lochlee, by Edzell, affording an opportunity of viewing the scenery of the North Esk, and of the range of the
Grampian mountains on the borders of Forfar and Aberdeen
shires. The distance is about 22 miles, and there is no inn in the
glen. EDZELL CASTLE was an old seat of the once powerful family
of Lindsay, and is now the property of the Earl of Dalhousie.
It is a beautiful architectural remnant, and the garden-wall is
ornamented by a number of elaborate carvings. Gannochy Bridge,
and The Burn (Colonel M'Inroy), about a mile north-east of
Edzell village, are romantic spots in the neighbourhood, and
favourite resorts for tourists. The drive may be continued to
the old kirkyard of Lochlee, where a monument has been erected
to Alexander Ross, author of *Lindy and Nory, or the Fortunate
Shepherdess*. From the Earl of Dalhousie's shooting-lodge of
Invermark there is a pony-road to Deeside, by Mount Keen, and
another from Tarfside to Charleston of Aboyne.

MONTROSE,

the last town in Forfarshire requiring notice, is a cheerful and
compact town built upon a narrow peninsula at the mouth of the
river South Esk, which here expands into a spacious basin, which
at high water has a striking effect. The High Street is a fine old
street, resembling in its architecture a Flemish town. It contains statues of the late Joseph Hume, who was born here in
1777, and Sir Robert Peel. Extensive links extend between the
burgh and the sea, affording ample scope for the game of golf.
The principal buildings are the town hall, the parish church,
Episcopal chapels, academy, museum of natural and antiquarian
objects, and the old lunatic asylum. The town is reached by a
branch railway line from Dubton Station, and carries on a considerable trade in shipping and linen manufacture. Among the
historical incidents connected with it is the embarkation of Sir
James Douglas for the Holy Land with the Heart of King

Robert Bruce. The Chevalier de St. George, son of the expatriated James II., disembarked here in 1715; and in the following year he returned to Montrose a fugitive, and next morning bade his last adieu to the country of his fathers. In the subsequent rising of 1745 it was for some time the head quarters of the Royalists; and in the river, between the town and village of Ferryden, the "Hazard" sloop of war was captured by Captain David Ferrier of Brechin, a notorious Jacobite. The famous Marquis of Montrose was born here in 1612. Montrose is distinguished as the first place in Scotland where the Greek language was taught; and here the learned scholar and divine, Andrew Melville, received his education. There are a number of gentlemen's seats and places of interest in the neighbourhood.

To the north of Forfarshire lies the county of Kincardine, the chief town of which is

STONEHAVEN,

now a favourite resort for sea-bathing, but chiefly interesting to the tourist for its vicinity to the castle of Dunnottar, anciently the seat of the Keiths, Earls Marischal, and which stands on a peninsulated rock 2 miles to the south. On three sides it is washed by the ocean, and towards the land is defended by a deep chasm. The only approach to it is by a steep path, winding round the body of the rock. During the reign of Charles II. this castle was used as a state prison for the Covenanters, who, without distinction, were packed into the "Whigs' Vault," a dungeon in front of a huge precipice, having a window open to the sea. They were treated by their keepers with the utmost rigour, and the walls still bear evidence of the severities inflicted upon them. "The Martyrs' Monument," which Paterson, the prototype of "Old Mortality," was engaged in renovating when he was first seen by Sir Walter Scott, stands in the churchyard of Dunnottar.

The first castle was built by Sir William Keith (about 1394), and the keep or donjon is supposed to be the oldest portion. During the Commonwealth Dunnottar was selected by the Scottish Parliament as the most secure depositary for the Regalia. The subsequent vicissitudes of these insignia of royalty, and all connected with them, form an interesting story which is well told by Sir Walter Scott in his *Provincial Antiquities of Scotland.*

ABERDEEN.

[*Hotels:* Imperial; Palace; Douglas's; Lemon Tree; Forsyth's Temperance.]

Aberdeen, "the granite city," ranks next to Edinburgh and Glasgow in point of general importance. Like the metropolis, it consists of an old and new town. Here, however, the old town is a mere suburb, and the new one the centre of business. The larger part of the town is situated on a cluster of eminences, under 100 feet above the sea-level, which rise along the northern bank of the river Dee, in the immediate vicinity of its confluence with the German Ocean. It is bounded on the south by the Dee, which is crossed by four bridges. One of these, of stone, is of considerable antiquity, having been begun by Bishop Elphinstone, and finished, about 1527, by Bishop Dunbar. The western or newer part of the city lies on an extensive flat, about 100 feet above the level of the sea, and is separated from the older part by the deep valley of the Denburn. All the principal streets are well built, and there prevails a general regularity of plan.

The principal street is UNION STREET, which extends about a mile in length, and contains most of the public buildings and hotels. It terminates eastwards at Castle Street, and presents a vista of greyish-white granite, of which the houses are almost exclusively constructed. On the north side of Union Street, opposite Market Street, is the Town and County Bank, having in its vicinity a marble statue of the Queen by the late Alexander Brodie, a native sculptor. A little farther west are the East and West churches, surrounded by a cemetery, which is separated from the street by an Ionic façade, each pillar being of a single stone. They are separated by Drum's Aisle, so called from its being the burial-place of the ancient family of Irvine of Drum, and which formed the transept of the original church of St. Nicholas, a fabric of the 12th century. The central tower, the only part remaining, and which contained a fine peal of bells, was burnt down in 1874. In the churchyard repose Dr. James Beattie (the author of *The Minstrel*), Principal Campbell, and the learned Blackwell. Union Street is carried over the Denburn valley by means of a bridge of one arch, 130 feet in span, and 50 feet high.

Close to the south-east corner of this bridge is the *Trades' Hall*, a fine granite structure, in which are some interesting portraits by Jameson and others, also a set of oak carved antique chairs, dating from 1574. Opposite is *Belmont Street*, leading north-wards, and containing a number of churches, including the South Church, a handsome granite building with a fine tower ; and the Free East, High, and South churches, which are conjoined in a cruciform building with a lofty brick spire of elegant style. Westward of the bridge, at the corner of Union Terrace, is the Northern Club, opposite to which stands a fine bronze statue of the late Prince Albert by Marochetti. At a little distance, along Union Street on the right, is the *Music Hall*. On the left is Crown Street, off which is the hand-some Episcopal chapel of St. John the Evangelist ; and in Huntly Street, on the right (off Union Street), is the Roman Catholic cathedral, a large and tasteful Gothic structure in granite, with a spire containing a peal of seven bells. Farther west is the Free West Church, a handsome Gothic edifice in Morayshire sandstone, with an elegant and lofty spire 175 feet high ; oppo-site, and a small way farther on, is the Free Gilcomston Church, a composite building of sandstone and granite, with a fine spire. At the extreme west end of Union Street stands the Free Church College. Beyond are Albyn Place and Rubislaw Terrace, the latter having spacious pleasure-grounds in front. North of these is St. Mary's Episcopal chapel.

From the south side of Union Street diverges MARKET STREET, leading to the quay and harbour and railway station. It con-tains the post-office and public markets, the latter being well worthy of a visit, especially on Friday, the market-day. The Mechanics' Institution, containing an excellent library and public hall for lectures, is on the left, and in the same building is the Government School of Design. In Hadden Street (off Market Street) is the Corn Exchange, a large building with an excellent Reading-room (admission 5s. a year, or 1d. each visit).

CASTLE STREET—the eastern portion of Union Street—is the *Place* of Aberdeen, and here are situated the *Town House* and Municipal Buildings, one of the largest and most imposing granite buildings in Scotland. On the opposite side of the street stands the Union Bank, a chaste building, and a little to the east Marischal Street branches off on the right. The military barracks occupy a commanding position on the site of the old castle of Aberdeen.

THE CROSS of Aberdeen stands in the centre of the upper end of Castle Street, and is adorned with large medallions of the Scottish monarchs, and surmounted by the royal unicorn rampant. A little in front of it stands a colossal granite statue of the last Duke of Gordon. In King Street are situated the Record Office (containing a portrait of the late Duke of Gordon by Lawrence), the Medical Hall, and St. Andrew's Episcopal church, in which there is a marble statue of Bishop Skinner by Flaxman ; also several banks.

Of the other public institutions may be named the Royal Infirmary at Woolmanhill ; the Lunatic Asylum, Rosemount ; the Asylum for the Blind in Huntly Street ; and Institution for Deaf and Dumb in Belmont Street. The Aberdeen Grammar School, famed for its antiquity, was removed from Schoolhill to an imposing edifice in Skene Street. Ross's School in Holborn Street is a neat decorated structure. Gordon's Hospital, in Schoolhill, resembles in character George Heriot's in Edinburgh ; and the Orphan Asylum, in Albyn Place, is a similar institution for females, which was built and endowed by Mrs. Elmslie, a native of Aberdeen, at a cost of £30,000.

There are some interesting examples of ancient street architecture in the Schoolhill, Gallowgate, Wallace Tower Nook, and Broad Street ; and in the last-named street the house is still shown where Lord Byron lived when a boy. The No. is 64.

MARISCHAL COLLEGE, the most important public institution in Aberdeen, is situated in Broad Street, and was founded by George Keith, Earl Marischal, in 1593. It is a massive granite structure, so completely buried among private buildings as to be visible only from its own court. The old buildings, which were mostly of the 17th century, were rebuilt, partly at the expense of Government and partly by subscription, at a cost of about £30,000. From the centre of the building springs a tower 100 feet high, containing the principal entry and the staircase leading to the Hall, Library, and Museum. In the square an obelisk of polished Peterhead granite, about 70 feet in height, is erected to the memory of Sir James Macgregor, a benefactor to the College.

Aberdeen possesses a good harbour, on the improvement of

which, together with the docks, large sums of money have been
expended. The pier is of great extent, and stretches into the
sea 2300 feet.

There are in Aberdeen and its vicinity extensive manufactories
of paper, wool, cotton, flax, jute, and iron, which employ
many thousand hands, and Aberdeen winceys are a specialty.
The polished granite stones, so famous for their durability and
beauty, form a staple export. Shipbuilding is carried on to a
considerable extent.

OLD ABERDEEN is about a mile to the north of the new city,
and near the mouth of the river Don. It is the seat of the
ancient college and cathedral, and boasts of great antiquity,
having received various privileges from Gregory the Great, a
monarch supposed to have died in the year 892. KING'S COLLEGE,
here situated, is a venerable edifice, founded in 1495 by Bishop
William Elphinstone of Aberdeen. The fabric is large and
stately, and is built in the form of a square, two sides of which
have been recently rebuilt. In the chapel, which is used for
public worship during session, there still remain the original
fittings of the choir. These are of most tasteful design and high
execution. The tower is vaulted with a double cross arch, surmounted by a sculptured crown, emblematical of the royal
support. In the chapel are to be seen the tombs of the founder,
and of Hector Boece, the first principal, and friend of Erasmus.
King's and Marischal Colleges were united in 1859. A little to
the north of the college is

The Cathedral of St. Machar, a noble structure, commenced
in 1366, whose antique spires and crowded burying-ground are
rich in time-worn sculpture. The nave is nearly perfect ; and
its western front (with two lofty spires), built of the obdurate
granite of the country, is stately in the severe symmetry of its
simple design. The choir seems never to have been finished ;
and of the transepts only the foundations now remain.

The BRIG OF BALGOWNIE, or *old Bridge of Don*, celebrated by
Lord Byron in the tenth canto of Don Juan, is about a mile from
Old Aberdeen.

The river Dee, which flows into the sea at Aberdeen, forms the
boundary between Aberdeen and Kincardine shires, and is distinguished by its beautiful wooded banks and valuable salmon-
fisheries. Its neighbour, the Don, rises on the confines of

Aberdeen and Banff shires, and is much less rapid, flowing, for a considerable part of its course, through rich valleys. According to an old rhyme—

> "Ae rood o' Don's worth twa o' Dee,
> Except it be for fish and tree."

Aberdeenshire has now attained the position of the best cattle-breeding county of Scotland. About a tenth part of the whole surface is under natural wood, chiefly of Scotch fir and birch, and the mountain forests abound in red deer, grouse, partridges, and other kinds of game.

ABERDEEN TO BALLATER AND BRAEMAR.
By Railway to Ballater, thence by Coach.

The valley of the Dee, or Deeside, as it is called, has long been a favourite route for tourists, principally on account of its being the highway to the wild scenery of Braemar. Few districts have been more favoured as places of residence, a fact attested not only by its having been selected by the Sovereign for her summer palace, but by the numerous castles' and mansions, ancient and modern, by which it is adorned.

The railway follows pretty closely the northern bank of the river, making a circuitous divergence to the north between Banchory and Aboyne. Near the latter stands Aboyne Castle, one of the seats of the Marquis of Huntly. There is a handsome suspension-bridge over the river here, and on the top of a hill near by an obelisk has been erected to the memory of the late Marquis of Huntly. The railway runs nearly due west from this for 8 miles, on the property of the Marquis of Huntly, and for the remainder of the route on that of Invercauld. We pass through the Muir of Dinnet, a monotonous district, relieved, however, by the opening prospect of the hills, which rise terrace-wise to the westward; and, highest of all, Lochnagar, the mountain monarch of the district. After crossing the Tullich water, and passing Monaltrie House, we reach

BALLATER,
[Hotel: Invercauld Arms.]

a favourite resort of visitors in the summer months; and, on account of its elevated position—660 feet above the sea—famed

for its healthy air. A bridge crosses the Dee to the chaly-
beate mineral wells of Pananich. A steep round knoll called
Craigendarroch, or the ·Rock of Oaks, rises right up from the
village to the height of 800 feet, and affords an extensive view.
Another rocky hill, 5 miles to the east, is frequently scaled on
account of Byron's couplet—

> "When I see some dark hill point its crest to the sky,
> I think on the rocks that o'ershadow Culbleen."

From like associations, the farm-house of Ballatrich, on the
south side of the river, where Byron lived, "rude as the rocks
where his infancy grew," is often visited. Five miles distant is
the Burn of the Vat, so termed on account of the water per-
forating a huge natural well in a perpendicular rock.

The great object of attraction is LOCHNAGAR, with its perennial
snows ; its summit is 3774 feet above the level of the sea, and
the ascent (which may also be made from Braemar or Crathie)
is considered about 12 miles in length. A part of Lord Byron's
early life was spent near this mountain, and the recollection of
that most "sublime and picturesque amongst our Caledonian
Alps," as he styles it, gave birth to some of his most beautiful
stanzas.

The road from Ballater to Braemar continues to follow the
north bank of the river. Skirting the base of Craigendarroch,
the Water of Gairn is crossed, and about a mile farther on, is
Craig Youzie (the Rock of Firs). Opposite the remains of a
pristine Highland clachan, called The Micras, is Abergeldie
Castle, the shooting-lodge of H.R.H. the Prince of Wales, where
the river is crossed by a rope-and-cradle bridge. A little beyond this is the village of Crathie with its parish church.
Opposite the post-office the river is crossed by an iron bridge,
which is the nearest approach to

BALMORAL CASTLE,

the Scottish summer residence of her Majesty. Balmoral Castle
is situated in a vale or dell formed by a range of high mountains.
The building is in the Scottish baronial style of architecture,
and was designed by William Smith, Esq., architect, of Aberdeen.

Passing INVER, we cross the bridge of Invercauld, thrown
over a rocky strait of the river, and soon after wind round the
foot of Craig Cluny. Beyond this the strath opens, showing

INVERCAULD HOUSE (Colonel Farquharson), the most beautifully
situated mansion on Deeside.   About the centre of the strath,
and on the south side of the river, is·Braemar Castle, a high
bare walled tower of modern erection.   Immediately beyond
is the

CASTLETON OF BRAEMAR.

a straggling collection of houses and huts built on a piece of
irregular ground, where the stream of Cluny rushes down to join
the Dee through a deep ravine.   The village contains two
excellent hotels, near one of which (the Invercauld Arms) the
Earl of Mar raised the standard of rebellion in 1715.; and
Established, Free, Episcopal, and Roman Catholic Churches.
The surrounding country is a region of deer-forests, and comprehends those of Mar, Ballochbowie, and Badenoch.
    The principal of the nearer excursions from Braemar comprise
the Falls of the Garrawalt (5 miles), Falls of Corriemulzie (3
miles), the Colonel's Bed, striking off at Inverey (5 miles), the
Linn of Quoich (3 miles), the Linn of Dee (6¼ miles).   The more
distant excursions are to Lochnagar (12 miles), Ben-muich-dhui
(20 miles), and to Ben-a-bourd.   The *Falls of the Garrawalt* are
5 miles east, on the declivity of the pine-forest of Ballochbowie,
and form a very attractive scene.   They are approached by passing Braemar Castle on the left, and turning off at the Bridge of
Invercauld, by the road to the right.   The Garrawalt water rolls
over several banks of considerable height, which, though not
perpendicular, create a thundering and foaming torrent.   A neat
wooden bridge crosses the stream, and conducts to a fog-house,
a favourite point of view.
    The Falls of Corriemulzie, and Linns of Quoich and Dee, are
also well worth visiting.   Near the last named, a new bridge
of granite was thrown across the river in 1857.

ABERDEEN TO INVERNESS.

By Great North of Scotland Railway.

No district of Scotland abounds more in ancient castellated
remains than Aberdeenshire and the adjacent counties of Banff,
Elgin, and Nairn.   Some of these are passed by this railway and

its branches, others are still not very accessible. Proceeding by the main line we reach Dyce Junction, where a branch railway strikes off into the district of Buchan. This district, of which Peterhead is the capital, is remarkable for the ruggedness of its coast-scenery, which includes the celebrated natural curiosity called the Bullers of Buchan. This lies about 6 miles to the south of Peterhead.

Near Inverurie is Keith Hall, the seat of the Earl of Kintore. About 3 miles from Inverurie, upon the steep rocky bank of a brook, stands the old square ruined tower of Balquhain, where Queen Mary spent two days in September 1562. At INVERAMSAY JUNCTION the branch-line to Turriff and Banff strikes off to the north, running pretty close to Fyvie Castle, one of the most interesting specimens in Scotland of the château or baronial style of architecture. Four miles north of Fyvie is the old castle of Towie Barclay, for many centuries the residence of the family of Barclay or Berkley.

Passing on the right Hatton Castle, we reach the town of TURRIFF, a place of some trade. Beyond this the railway skirts the right side of the Deveron to

BANFF,

an ancient royal burgh, situated at the mouth of the same river, and containing several handsome public buildings. The castle of Banff was once a residence of the Earls of Seafield, and in it was born the unfortunate Archbishop Sharp. Near Banff is the picturesque bridge of Alvah ; also the ruins of Inchdrewer Castle, in which George, third Lord Banff, was burned to death in 1713. In the immediate neighbourhood is Duff House, the magnificent mansion of the Earl of Fife, containing some valuable paintings, and surrounded by an extensive park.

Pursuing the main line from Inveramsay, after passing Logie Elphinstone, Pitcaple House, and the hill of Benachie, we reach the village of OYNE, where there is a view of the valley of the Gaudy, famous in Scotch song. Near INSCH station is the village of Rothney, and in the vicinity is the conical hill of

Dunnideer, upon which are the remains of an old castle. The line runs along Bogieside to the town of HUNTLY, where a statue has been erected to the late Duke of Richmond. On the south side is Scott's Hospital, for the reception of aged persons. In the vicinity are the ruins of Huntly Castle, a fine old fabric, built by George, first Marquis of Huntly. The modern residence of Huntly Lodge was the residence of the late Duchess of Gordon, who erected the gateway in honour of her husband.

Passing Rothiemay village, and along the valley of the Isla, we gain the populous town of KEITH. Near the station may be seen the ruins of Castle Oliphant.

At Keith we cross the Spey, which here forms the boundary between Banff and Elgin shires. The stations of Orton Junction * and Fochabers are passed in succession, from the last of which FOCHABERS village is 3 miles distant. At the west end of the village a handsome arch forms the entrance to *Castle Gordon*, the seat of the Duke of Richmond. Soon after this we reach the Cathedral town of

ELGIN,

[*Hotel:* Gordon Arms.]

the principal town of Elgin or Morayshire. In construction it resembles many other towns in Scotland, where a main or High Street forms the backbone from which numerous alleys diverge. It is surrounded by a beautiful country, which may be well viewed from the summit of Ladyhill, an eminence on the west of the city, on which a column has been erected to the memory of the last Duke of Gordon. The principal object of attraction in Elgin is the Cathedral, which was founded in 1223, during the time of Bishop Moray, and dedicated to the Holy Trinity. It has been at one time covered with a profusion of sculpture, but, like most buildings of the kind in Scotland, it is much dilapidated.

The principal entrance is on the west side, between the

---

* Six miles south from Orton Junction, and connected by a branch line with Craigellachie, is the village of ROTHES, situated on a plain, upon which the lofty Benrinnes, the most northerly of the Grampian chain, looks down. Near the west end of the village stand the ruins of the castle of Rothes, once the seat of the Leslies, Earls of Rothes.

bulky masses of the western towers, which are 84 feet in height.
The encircling arch of this grand entrance presents some beautiful and delicately-chiselled ornaments, in a much earlier style
of architecture than the recorded date of the foundation. The
decorations of the turrets on the east, and of certain of the
pilasters, exhibit good specimens of later art. The most complete part of the building is the *Chapter-house* on the north-east, or, as it is called from a tradition, the "'Prentice Aisle."
Between this and the north cloister is the lavatory.

Passing from these we enter the *Choir*, then the *Chancel*
with its splendid double row of lancet-windows, under which
stood the high altar and tomb of the founder. Adjoining,
and entered by a gate, is St. Mary's Aisle, the burial-place of
the ducal family of Gordon. There are several other tombs of
interest, including one of the first Marquis of Huntly, and
Bishop Winchester. Among several interesting fragments of
statues, one is said to represent Bishop Innes, the founder of the
now lost middle tower.. A broken stone coffin is shown as that
in which the body of King Duncan was buried.

The environs of Elgin contain several very interesting antiquities. About 4 miles to the north-east, upon the margin of
a loch, stand the ruins of Spynie Palace, formerly a fortified
residence of the Bishops of Moray. On the other side of Elgin,
in a sheltered valley about 6 miles south-west, are the ruins of

Pluscarden Priory,

founded by Alexander II. in 1230, and dedicated to St. Andrew.
The building had been partly in the first, partly in the second,
Pointed styles. Only a fragment of the south wall of the nave
remains; but the choir, which is nearly 57 feet long, is in pretty
good preservation, as well as the chapter-house, which is a
square, with enriched roof, supported by a central clustered
pillar. The refectory (now used as a place of worship), the
dormitories, kitchen, and other apartments, together with a
few tombstones, and the fine old orchard, are worthy of note.
The tourist may return from his visit to Pluscarden, by the
Romanesque church of Birnie.

Proceeding from Elgin to Inverness, and approaching nearer
to the Moray Firth, we reach the railway junction and town of

FORRES,

containing a good hotel (Campbell's Royal Station), and a large Hydropathic Establishment. The town is situated near the mouth of the river Findhorn, and consists mostly of one long street, the chief features of which are its pointed gables and low Saxon doorways. The most prominent buildings are the jail and court-house and town-cross.

A mile and a half to the east of the town stands the famous Forres Pillar or "Sweno's Stone," which is about twenty feet high, and is carved with figures of warriors and other objects; the general opinion being that it was raised in the reign of Malcolm II. to commemorate the final expulsion of the Danes.

Crossing the Findhorn we proceed on our journey to Nairn, passing Brodie House, the ancient seat of the family of this name. Near this is Hardmoor, the traditional meeting-place of Macbeth and Banquo with the witches. About a mile southwards is the Earl of Moray's mansion of Darnaway Castle.

We next reach the ancient royal burgh of

NAIRN,
[Royal Marine Hotel.]

situated on the Moray Firth, at the mouth of the river Nairn, 15¼ miles east from Inverness. It contains several public buildings, and numerous handsome private residences. The town is resorted to in summer for sea-bathing.

About 5 miles to the south of it stands Cawdor Castle, interesting alike from its architecture and historic associations. It is in excellent preservation, being used as a summer residence by the Earl of Cawdor. The entrance is by a drawbridge thrown across a dry moat. There is a legend that King Duncan was murdered here by Macbeth, but it is wholly without foundation.

On leaving Nairn we enter Inverness-shire near Fort-George. The railway skirts the shore of the Firth of Inverness, and passes to the north of Culloden Moor. This, as well as Inverness, which is reached shortly afterwards, are described on a subsequent page (124).

GLASGOW.

[*Hotels*: St. Enoch's, Station; Queen's; Grand; Maclean's; Mac-rae's; Royal; George; Crown; Hanover; North British; Victoria; Bedford's; Steel's. *Temperance*: Washington; Waverley. *Restaurants*: Lang's, 73 Queen Street; Ferguson and Forrester's, 36 Buchanan Street.]

GLASGOW, the commercial metropolis of Scotland, and the third city in the United Kingdom in point of wealth, population, and commercial importance, is situated in Lanarkshire, on the river Clyde, at a point whence that river becomes navigable to the Atlantic Ocean. It is the most populous town in Scotland, the number of its inhabitants, according to the last census, of 1871, being, in round numbers, 478,000.

The reputed founder of Glasgow was St. Kentigern, or St. Mungo as he is familiarly termed, who came from the Orkney Islands to preach the Gospel to the Strathclyde Britons in the year 539. Since the days of Charles I. Glasgow has been a stronghold of Presbyterianism, and the famous Assembly by which Episcopacy was abolished was held in this city in 1638.

In a commercial point of view Glasgow has shown the most extraordinary progress. In addition to the manufacture of cotton goods, to which Glasgow largely owes her pre-eminence, there have been more recently developed the coal and iron trades, along with steamboat building and marine engine making. Indeed the shipbuilding of the Clyde exceeds that of all the other ports of Great Britain combined. The chemical works of St. Rollox are understood to be the largest in the world. To the labours and discoveries of Watt and Bell, Glasgow is largely indebted for her prominent position as a manufacturing and commercial community, and monuments to perpetuate their memory have been erected by their grateful fellow-citizens. That of the former is placed in George Square, in the centre of the city; the latter at Dunglas on the Clyde, on a commanding situation 11 miles below Glasgow.

The progress of Glasgow as a port has been mainly promoted by the extensive widening and deepening operations which have been effected on the Clyde. The length of quay-wall in the harbour now exceeds 17,000 feet, and along this vessels are constantly ranged three and four abreast, in addition to others moored in mid-channel.

ARGYLE STREET

is the principal street of Glasgow, and, taken in its whole extent from east to west, it exhibits a continuous line at least three miles in length. The prevailing character of the buildings is plain, and there is no attempt at uniformity of arrangement. A few ancient tenements, with narrow-pointed gables and steep roofs, here and there attract the eye, and form a contrast to the modern elegance of the shops beneath. At the Trongate, the Tron Steeple, a venerable-looking spire, projects nearly the whole breadth of the pavement. A little farther on is the *Cross*, forming a centre, whence various streets, including the High Street, Gallowgate, London Street, and Saltmarket, diverge. There is placed here an equestrian statue of William the Third. The ancient burgh Jail, the scene of the midnight adventure of Francis Osbaldistone and Rob Roy, stood exactly at the corner of the High Street and Trongate—a site now occupied by a heavy pile of shops and warehouses. The *Town-Hall* and the Cross Steeple still survive as relics of the ancient civic splendour of this part of the city.

BUCHANAN STREET is famed for the elegance of its shops. It contains the Western Club, and at its northern extremity is the principal station of the Caledonian Railway. An *Arcade* connects it on the west with Argyle Street. *Queen Street* may be said to be the next in importance to Buchanan Street, which it much resembles. Here is situated THE ROYAL EXCHANGE, a handsome building containing an extensive news-room, to which there is free admittance. In front of the building stands an equestrian statue of the Duke of Wellington by Marochetti. On the north, Queen Street opens into GEORGE SQUARE, the finest and most central square in the city: It is ornamented by several monuments, of which the most striking are Sir Walter Scott's, Queen Victoria's and the late Prince Consort's, Sir John Moore's and Lord Clyde's (the last two having been natives of Glasgow), James Watt's, Sir Robert Peel's, and Robert Burns's. A number of public buildings, banks, etc., are clustered in this vicinity, including the *General Post Office*, the *North British*

Railway Station, the *Athenæum*, *High School*, and *Andersonian University*.

HIGH STREET—OLD COLLEGE—CATHEDRAL.

From the east end of Argyle Street, here called the Trongate, the *High Street* diverges to the north, like the backbone of the ancient city. Beyond Duke Street it ascends, with a considerable curve, what is called the "Bell of the Brae," becoming at this point rather steep and narrow. At the top, the most ancient part of the city, is situated

The Cathedral.

(Admittance every day, from 10 A.M. to 6 P.M. On Tuesdays and
Thursdays there is a charge of 2d. each.
Divine service on Sundays at 11 A.M. and 2 P.M.)

This fine old minster was founded by John Achaius, Bishop of Glasgow, in 1133, in the reign of David I. The architecture is of a massive, rather than elegant style of Gothic ; but its peculiar character is well suited to its position and surroundings.

Originally it consisted of three churches, one of which, the Old Barony, occupied the crypt, and was called the Laigh Kirk. Here Scott lays the scene of Rob Roy's mysterious warning to Francis Osbaldistone. The building is in length, from east to west, 319 feet ; in width, 63 feet, and the spire is 225 feet high.

THE CATHEDRAL WINDOWS.

In the year 1856 it was resolved by a committee of citizens to enhance the beauty of the edifice by a series of stained-glass windows, to be executed on a concerted scheme of illustration. Several of these were accordingly erected at the expense of private individuals ; but the local effort being countenanced by Government, the eastern window (one of the finest of the series) was defrayed by a grant. When the whole were finished, numbering 81, they were formally presented to the Crown. The windows in the nave, transepts, and Lady Chapel, were all executed at the royal establishment of glass-painting in Munich ; those in the chapter-house and crypts by various British and foreign artists, whose names, as well as those of the donors, are given in a descriptive catalogue sold in the Cathedral. The subjects are arranged with a certain regard to chronological order, commencing, at the N.W. corner of the nave, with the expulsion of Adam and Eve from Paradise, and continued to the S.W. angle with other Old Testament characters. The *great west window* contains subjects taken from the history of the Jews ; and the *north transept window* figures of the prophets and John the Baptist. The subjects in *the choir* illustrate the parables ; those in the *Lady Chapel* are figures of the apostles ; and those in the *great eastern window*, the evangelists.

THE NECROPOLIS,

which forms the great cemetry of Glasgow, covers an eminence rising steeply to a height of from 200 to 300 feet above the Cathedral. The surface of the rock is divided into walks bristling with columns, with every variety of monumental erections, some of them peculiarly beautiful and chaste in design. John Knox's monument rises above all the others from the summit of this hill of tombs (some 250 feet above the level of the Clyde), where the spectator may survey one of the most striking and varied of city scenes.

WEST END OF THE CITY.

The principal street on the north side of Glasgow is *Sauchiehall Street*, and it is the main avenue to the west end. Here are situated the Corporation Galleries, containing an extensive collection of ancient paintings, acquired by the Corporation chiefly from the estate of the late Archibald M'Lellan, Esq. They also contain a marble statue of William Pitt by Chantrey, and other objects of art. At Charing Cross a bronze statue of the late James Oswald, M.P. for Glasgow, has been erected. This vicinity is noted for its numerous handsome ecclesiastical structures.

At the western extremity of Sauchiehall Street are various Terraces and Crescents, which form the residences of the local aristocracy. The highly picturesque lands of Woodlands and Kelvin Grove, occupying the east bank of the Kelvin, were purchased by the Corporation at a cost of nearly £100,000, and now form "The West-end Park." The ground was laid out by the late Sir Joseph Paxton, and includes the "Kelvin Grove," commemorated in the well-known song of that name. Here we reach Gilmore Hill, on the summit of which is situated

THE UNIVERSITY OF GLASGOW,

a building of which the city may be justly proud, and which in every respect presents a striking contrast to the original monastic structure it has recently replaced.

The building was designed by the late Sir Gilbert Scott, the celebrated architect, in the general style of Early English architecture, intermixed with the best forms of Scoto-French domestic and secular style of a somewhat later period. It is surmounted by a central tower 300 feet in height. The foundation-stone was laid by the Prince and Princess of Wales in 1868, and the opening ceremonial took place in 1870. Each chair has allotted to it a distinct class-room with retiring room, and all the suitable laboratories and apparatus rooms, when necessary. A very large public reading-room has been provided for the students, in close proximity to the library.

The Museum includes that founded by the celebrated Dr. Hunter, who studied at Glasgow. It consists of a splendid collection of books, coins, paintings, and anatomical preparations, which has been valued at £130,000.

The Botanic Garden is situated in this vicinity, and contains the KIBBLE CRYSTAL ART PALACE, a large glass building devoted to the recreation of the people. The observatory occupies a lofty eminence south-west of the garden.

The buildings of Blythswood Square form one of the finest and most prominent objects to the stranger approaching Glasgow from the west. In the south-west corner of this square is the Episcopal church of St. Jude's, in the Egyptian style of architecture.

RAILWAY STATIONS.

Glasgow is well supplied with railway stations, the principal of which are as follows :—

St. Enoch's Station (and hotel), occupying a convenient position in St. Enoch's Square, opposite the south end of Buchanan Street. This is the station of the Union Railway, including the Glasgow and South-Western Railway. The Caledonian Railway has three stations—1, *The Central* in Gordon Street, connected with 2, Bridge Street Station, by a new bridge crossing the Clyde parallel with Glasgow Bridge ; 3, Buchanan Street. The North British Railway Station is in Queen Street ; and there is another, the College Station, in High Street.

THE BROOMIELAW,

or harbour of Glasgow, comprises an area of 76 acres. It is upwards of 400 feet wide, and more than a mile and a half in length. The quays along each side accommodate vessels of every description, from the largest ships to the smallest coasting craft. Steam-vessels are to be seen here at all hours discharging or receiving crowds of passengers. A walk of about half-a-mile eastwards from the Broomielaw by the bank of the river brings the tourist to

GLASGOW GREEN,

the oldest public park in Glasgow, and the area on which the annual *Fair* is held in the month of July. It is diversified with walks, some of which are shaded by trees, and is surrounded by a carriage-drive about two miles and a quarter in extent. From an obelisk, erected to the memory of Nelson, Glasgow appears to great advantage ; the landscape includes the various bridges and the long ranges of buildings on the banks of the river. On the west of the Green are the Court-houses and Jail, and to the south of these is the *Albert Bridge*, a new structure of remarkable beauty. Near it is the massive bridge by which the Union Railway crosses the Clyde. Farther down the river is crossed by the Victoria and Glasgow suspension bridges.

SOUTH SIDE.

The portion of the city on the south side of the Clyde comprises various districts, with a population exceeding 100,000. It contains some extensive locomotive engine and malleable iron works ; and others where the processes of spinning, weaving, dyeing, and calico-printing are carried on upon a vast scale. The docks and shipbuilding yards of Glasgow on both sides of the river westwards, down to Govan, are among the remarkable sights of Glasgow.

The *Queen's* or *South-side Park* is a magnificent piece of ground upwards of 100 acres in extent, upon which a large sum has been expended. It is approached by one of the handsomest thoroughfares in the city, extending for a mile nearly in a straight line from Argyle Street to the flag-staff at the summit of the park. Closely adjoining the park is *Langside*, where Queen Mary met with her final defeat in 1568.

The water with which Glasgow is supplied is obtained from Loch Katrine, a distance of 40 miles. It is of almost unequalled purity, and furnishes nearly 50 gallons per head daily.

EXCURSIONS FROM GLASGOW.

The large manufacturing town of

PAISLEY

is situated in Renfrewshire, on the banks of the White Cart, a tributary of the Clyde, 7 miles from Glasgow. In the square visible from the railway are the County Buildings, containing the court-house, jail, etc. There are several public buildings, including a handsome Free Library, presented to the town by Sir Peter Coats. The Abbey Church of Paisley was founded about the year 1163 by Walter Stuart, ancestor of the royal family of Scotland, and dedicated to St. James and St. Mirren. The chancel remains entire, and is used as a parish church. Attached to the south side is a small but lofty chapel, containing the tomb of Marjory, daughter of Robert Bruce, and wife of the founder. This lady, the mother of Robert II., first of the Stuart line, was killed by a fall from her horse in the neighbourhood. The buildings connected with the abbey are now the property of the Duke of Abercorn, the representative of Claud Hamilton, the last abbot and first temporal superior. Adjoining the town is an extensive public park, 7½ acres in extent, which was presented to the inhabitants by Thomas Coats, Esq., of Ferguslie.

Paisley has given birth to two celebrated men of the name of Wilson, one the American Ornithologist, the other the Professor and author of the *Isle of Palms*. It is also the native place of the Scottish poet Tannahill. About half-way between Glasgow and Paisley are the ruins of Crookston Castle, the *maison de plaisance* where Queen Mary was betrothed to Darnley. Not far from Crookston is Hawkhead House, a seat of the Earl of Glasgow.

HAMILTON AND BOTHWELL CASTLE.

(North British College Station. Several trains daily each way.)

Hamilton is the capital of the Middle Ward of Lanarkshire, and an ancient parliamentary burgh, carrying on a considerable trade in weaving and tambouring. It is situated in the midst of an iron and coal district, and notwithstanding this apparently adverse element, it is noted for its fruit and flower gardens.

HAMILTON PALACE, the seat of the Duke of Hamilton and Brandon, stands on a plain between the town and the river. It is a large classical building, with a projecting pillared portico, after the style of the Temple of Jupiter Stator at Rome, 264 feet in length and 60 feet in height. The pillars of the portico (12 in number), each formed of a solid block of stone, are 25 feet high, and fully 10 feet in span. The interior of the palace, which is not generally shown, contains a number of costly works of art and virtu. Among other pictures, Rubens' "Daniel in the Lions' Den " is to be seen here.

About two miles to the south-east of Hamilton is Cadzow Castle, the original residence of the Hamilton family. It occupies a romantic site, overhanging the Avon, and is surrounded by part of the old Caledonian Forest, where still roam the celebrated white breed of Scottish wild cattle. Sir Walter Scott has made Cadzow Castle the subject of a spirited ballad.

Nearly opposite Cadzow, and connected with the palace by a magnificent avenue, is the ancient château of Chatelherault.

On the banks of the South Calder, at no great distance from Hamilton, there are a number of family seats, including Dalziel House (Major Hamilton, M.P.), built 1649 ; Wishaw House (late Lord Belhaven) ; Coltness (H. Holdsworth, Esq.) ; Allanton (Sir H. J. S. Steuart, Bart.) ; Cleland (Lord Stair) ; Carfin (R. Steuart, Esq.) ; Orbiston (late Mrs. Douglas). On the river Rotten Calder, parish of Blantyre, there are also a number of fine seats, among which is Calderwood Castle (Sir W. M. Maxwell), worthy of a visit for the picturesque character of its grounds. On the North Calder is Woodhall, and on the Avon, Fairholm (J. Hamilton, Esq.) At Strathavon are the ruins of the fine old castle of Avondale, where the good Duchess Anne Hamilton found shelter. In this parish is Drumclog, where the Covenanters defeated Claverhouse in 1679. An annual sermon is still preached on the field of battle on 1st June.

In the vicinity of Hamilton are the clipped terraced gardens of Barncluith, constructed originally by an ancestor of Lord Belhaven, about 1583, and now the property of Lady Ruthven. Bothwell Bridge, which crosses the Clyde two miles north of Hamilton, is the scene of the famous battle, fought in 1679, between the Royal forces, under the Duke of Monmouth, and the Covenanters. The bridge has been much altered, but a part of the ancient structure still remains. The reader may be reminded of the spirited description given of this engagement in Scott's novel of "Old Mortality," as well as in the ballad contained in his "Minstrelsy of the Scottish Border."

A little farther on we reach the village of

BOTHWELL,

now one of the fashionable resorts of the Glasgow merchants, but principally noted for the picturesque ruins of its Castle,* which stand on the right bank of the Clyde, about a mile distant. The building is a noble relic of Norman architecture, and consists of a large oblong quadrangle, flanked towards the south by two huge circular towers, and covering an area of 234 feet in length and 99 feet in breadth. Some parts of the walls are 14 feet thick and 60 feet in height. The fosse can still be traced, and so also may the flying buttresses and ramparts. The chapel at the east end, or rather part of it, is recognised by the shafted windows, as the font, altar, stance, etc., are in the open space beyond. A circular dungeon, 24 feet by 12, called Wallace's Beef-barrel, is still shown. The Clyde here makes a beautiful sweep, and forms the semicircular declivity celebrated in Scottish song as Bothwell Bank. The best view of the ruins is obtained from a fog-house on the river's brink. The Castle is the property of the Countess of Home.

* Tourists admitted by the principal gateway only on Tuesdays and Fridays, from 11 A.M. to 4 P.M., and expected to retire from the grounds before 6 o'clock. No admission other days.

THE FALLS OF THE CLYDE.

[This romantic scene may be visited with almost equal convenience from
  Glasgow or from Edinburgh, being from the former 25, and from the
  latter 32 miles distant. In either case the tourist takes his ticket for
  Lanark, where is a good hotel, the CLYDESDALE. Here a ticket and
  guide are obtained at a small charge, each party 1s. for two hours,
  and 6d. for every additional half-hour. The distance from the first
  gate to the last fall is 1½ mile.]

The town of Lanark is interesting as the scene of many of
Wallace the Scottish patriot's exploits, and a statue of the hero
is placed in a niche above the entrance to the parish church.

In visiting the Falls from Lanark the tourist proceeds first to
CORA LINN, the largest, where the river takes three distinct
leaps, and falls altogether a height of about 84 feet. The best
view of this magnificent fall is from the semicircular seat on the
verge of the opposite cliff. It may also be viewed with advantage from the bottom. Above the fall, a pavilion is fitted up
with mirrors, so arranged as to give the water the appearance of
being precipitated upon the spectator. Here also are the old
castle of Cora, and Corehouse, the seat of the late Lord Corehouse.*

From Cora Linn the tourist proceeds by a romantic path to
BONNINGTON LINN (the uppermost fall, two miles from Lanark),
passing through the grounds of Bonnington, the seat of Sir
Charles Ross. In Bonnington House are preserved two relics
of Sir William Wallace—a portrait, and a curious chair on which
he is said to have sat. Above the cataract the river moves very
slowly, but all at once it bends towards the north-west, and,
dividing its current on either side, throws itself over a perpendicular rock of about 30 feet into a deep basin.

STONEBYRES, the largest fall, is about 4 miles below Lanark.
The river here is broader, and rushes over its precipitous bed
with great grandeur. Stonebyres House (General Douglas) is
in the neighbourhood. There is no good access to the fall, and
the scrambling steps, called "*Jacob's Ladder*," which conduct

* About half-a-mile below Cora Linn is the village of New Lanark,
founded in the year 1783 by the benevolent David Dale of Glasgow, father-
in-law of Robert Owen. The village contains about 2500 inhabitants, who
are engaged in the adjoining cotton-spinning mills.

to the channel of the river, must be avoided by those who have not sufficiently strong nerves. A guide is generally ready to render his services.

Cartland Crags and Wallace's Cave form a romantic scene on the Mouse Water, about a mile north-west from Lanark. The stream flows through a deep chasm, formed apparently by an earthquake, where the rocks rise to a height of nearly 400 feet. A bridge is thrown across this ravine, consisting of three arches, 128 feet in height. A short distance beneath is an old bridge, supposed to be of Roman origin. On the north side of the stream, a few yards above the new bridge, is the Cave where Wallace took refuge after he had slain Haselrig, the English sheriff. Jerviswood, the ancient seat of the illustrious John Baillie, who was murdered under the forms of law during the reign of Charles II., is about a mile and a half northward from Lanark.

In a picturesque valley about 3 miles northward of Lanark is situated Lee House, the seat of Sir Simon Macdonald Lockhart, Bart., where there is still kept the famous talismanic coin called Lee Penny, the use made of which by Sir Walter Scott in his novel of "The Talisman" may be familiar to the reader. The ruins of Craignethan Castle, the prototype of the "Tillietudlem" of "Old Mortality," are a few miles to the north-west, on the way to Hamilton.

AYR AND THE LAND OF BURNS.

The town of Ayr is situated on the sea-coast, at the mouth of the river Ayr, and contains a number of handsome public buildings, and some good hotels, including The King's Arms, Queen's, and Ayr Arms. The river, which divides Ayr proper from Newtown and Wallacetown, is crossed by two bridges, termed respectively the Auld and New Brigs—noticed under these denominations by Burns in his poem of "The Twa Brigs." The Auld Brig is said to have been built in the reign of Alexander III. (1249-1285) by two maiden sisters of the name of Low, whose effigies were consequently carved upon a stone in the eastern parapet, near the south end of the fabric. The new bridge was erected in 1788, chiefly through the exertions of Provost Ballantyne, the gentleman to whom Burns dedicated

his poem. A Gothic structure erected on the site of the tower
in which Wallace was confined, contains the clock and bells of
the Dungeon steeple, and is ornamented by a statue of the hero.
Another statue of Wallace has been placed in front of a house
occupying the site of the ancient court-house, where, according
to Blind Harry, the Scottish Lords were treacherously hanged.
A few fragments remain of the fort of Ayr built by Oliver Cromwell in 1652, and an old tower, which formed part of St. John's
Church, founded in the 12th century, has been fitted up as a
modern residence.

About 14 miles to the north of Ayr is Kilwinning, a small town
with some 3000 inhabitants, chiefly engaged in the surrounding
mineral works. The place takes its name from the Saint Winnin
who settled here at an early period, and gave rise to the monastery subsequently founded by Hugh de Moreville in 1140. The
remains of the Abbey subsequently erected consist mainly of
the south transept, which is a beautiful fragment of the First
Pointed style. Near Kilwinning is Eglinton Castle, the seat of
the Earl of Eglinton and Wintoun. In the surrounding park the
famous Eglinton Tournament took place in 1839.

The sea-coast to the north of Ayr is flat and sandy. Southwards it becomes bold and rocky, projecting into the well-
known landmarks called the "Heads of Ayr." On either
side, within a few miles, are the ruins of Greenan, and Dunure
Castles, in the latter of which the Commendator of Cross-
raguel Abbey* was roasted alive before a slow fire by the Earl
of Cassilis.

Colzean, or Colyean Castle, the principal seat of the Marquis
of Ailsa, is situated about 2 miles from the village of Kirk-
oswald. This magnificent mansion stands upon the verge of a
massive basaltic cliff overhanging the sea, and presents a range
of lofty castellated buildings with Gothic windows. It contains
an extensive and valuable collection of arms and armour.

Directly underneath the castle are the Coves of Colzean, which,
according to popular report, are a favourite haunt of fairies. A
few miles to the south stand the ruins of Turnberry Castle—

* The ruins of this Abbey are 2 miles from Maybole. It was founded by
Duncan, first Earl of Carrick, about the year 1240, and was a dependency of
the Abbey of Paisley.

"Where Bruce once ruled the martial ranks,
And shook his Carrick spear"—

and which, during the 12th and 13th centuries, was the principal seat of the Earls of Carrick. Robert Bruce, King of Scotland, if not born in Turnberry Castle, must have spent many of his youthful years in it, and it was here that a fire, accidentally kindled, was mistaken by him for an appointed signal to attempt the deliverance of his country.

Opposite this part of the coast, at a distance of 10 miles, is Ailsa Craig, a huge rocky island, 2 miles in circumference, which rises abruptly from the sea to the height of 1103 feet. Its nearest distance to land is about 10 miles. Upon its summit are the ruins of a tower of three storeys. It is the property of the Marquis of Ailsa, who takes from it his title as a British peer.

BURNS'S BIRTHPLACE AND MONUMENT, AND ALLOWAY KIRK.

All admirers of Burns will be gratified with a visit to his birthplace, and the scenes in the neighbourhood with which he is associated. This may be easily accomplished from Ayr.

Taking the road southwards by way of Alloway Kirk, we come upon various localities mentioned in "Tam o' Shanter," including

"The ford,
Where in the snaw the chapman smoored;"

and a little farther on,

"The meikle stane,
Where drucken Charlie brak's neck-bane."

Passing the mansion of Roselle, at the distance of about 2 miles from Ayr, we reach

BURNS'S COTTAGE,

where the poet was born on the 25th January 1759. The original erection was a clay bigging, consisting of two apartments, the kitchen and the spence or sitting-room. The cottage remains somewhat in its pristine condition; and in the interior of the kitchen is shown a recess where the birth took place.

On an eminence, about a mile and a half to the south-east of the cottage, stands the farm of Mount Oliphant, which Burns's father rented on leaving the cottage.

H

Proceeding towards Burns's monument, we pass by

"𝔄𝔩𝔩𝔬𝔴𝔞𝔭'𝔰 𝔞𝔲𝔩𝔡 𝔥𝔞𝔲𝔫𝔱𝔢𝔡 𝔎𝔦𝔯𝔨,"

with its now roofless walls, but still retaining its old belfry. In the area of the kirk the late Lord Alloway, one of the Judges of the Court of Session, is interred ; and near the gate of the churchyard is the grave of Burns's father. A new church has been erected in the neighbourhood.

In the immediate vicinity of Alloway Kirk are the modern mansion of Cambusdoon (Mrs. Baird), and Newark Castle, an old seat of the Marquis of Ailsa.

A few hundred yards from the Kirk is the "Auld Brig" of Doon, which figures so conspicuously in the tale of "Tam o' Shanter." Directly over the New Bridge stands

BURNS'S MONUMENT,

a classical building, erected in 1820 from a cyclostylar design by the late Thomas Hamilton of Edinburgh. In an apartment on the ground-floor there are exhibited here several appropriate articles—various editions of the poet's works, a snuff-box made from the wood-work of Alloway Kirk, a copy of the original portraits of Burns by Nasmyth, etc., and the Bible given by Burns to his Highland Mary. From the base of the columns a view is obtained of the surrounding grounds, which are tastefully laid out, and include a grotto containing statues of Tam o' Shanter and Souter Johnny.

The Doon, to which the writings of Burns have given such celebrity, rises in a lake of the same name, about 8 miles in length, situated in the great mineral district of Dalmellington. It has a seaward course of 18 miles, throughout which it amply sustains its right to the title of "Bonnie Doon."

DUMFRIESSHIRE AND SOUTH-WEST OF SCOTLAND.

The country to the south of Lanark, through which the Caledonian Railway passes, has a fresh and green aspect, although it is occasionally bleak and uninteresting. The railway follows the river Clyde almost to its source.

The first station of importance, after leaving Carstairs, is

Symington Junction, where a branch line is carried eastwards to Biggar and Peebles, by which the tourist may follow the banks of the Tweed from near its source to where it joins the sea. The fine conical-shaped hill on the west is Tinto, which rises to the height of 2200 feet. Proceeding southward, we pass Lamington, the seat of Baillie Cochrane, Esq., and Abington, that of Sir T. E. Colebrooke, Bart. At Elvanfoot we are within five or six miles of the mining villages of Leadhills and Wanlockhead, which occupy lofty situations amid the Lowther Hills on the west. As the name betokens, lead is found here in considerable quantities. Shortly after leaving Elvanfoot we cross the watershed of the Clyde and Annan, reaching the main stream of the latter at Beattock. Two miles to the east of this station is

MOFFAT,

an agreeably situated watering-place, deservedly famed for the efficacy of its mineral waters. The village consists mainly of one broad and well-built street, in which are the two principal hotels (the Annandale and Buccleuch Arms), the reading-room, etc. The well-house is situated on the side of a beautiful linn, a mile and a half from the village, and may be reached by omnibuses which leave the hotels every morning.* The water of this spring is sulphureous, and has, when newly drawn, a slightly disagreeable smell, though it is beautifully clear and cool. Moffat is surrounded by mountains, among which is the Hartfell group, the highest in the south of Scotland, ranging from 2000 to 2600 feet. The principal seats in the neighbourhood are—Raehills (Hope Johnstone, Esq., of Annandale), Auchen Castle (Hon. H. Butler Johnstone), Dumcrieff (Lord Rollo).

An excursion may be made from Moffat to the Grey Mare's Tail and St. Mary's Loch, to which stage-coaches run on certain days of the week in connection with the morning and evening trains, and return. The *Grey Mare's Tail* is one of the finest waterfalls in Scotland, and nearly 200 feet high. The name is doubtless derived from the resemblance of the fall to the tail of a horse, being, as Scott describes it,

* A large Hydropathic Establishment affords further attractions for residence in this neighbourhood.

> " White as the snowy charger's tail."

The stream has its source in Loch Skene, a wild and desolate
tarn about two miles to the westward. A short way north of
this we reach the source of the Yarrow, which, after a short
course, forms the Loch o' the Lowes, and then falls into St.
Mary's Loch.

On a grassy knoll to the left stands a monument of James
Hogg, the Ettrick Shepherd.

There is a good Inn here (Tibbie Shiels's), a favourite resort of
anglers. St. Mary's Loch is 16 miles from Moffat, and about
the same distance from Selkirk. It is remarkable for the
simple character of its scenery :—

> "Abrupt and sheer the mountains sink
> At once upon the level brink ;
> And just a trace of silver sand
> Marks where the water meets the land."
>
> *Marmion.*

Proceeding from Beattock through Annandale, we follow
pretty closely the banks of the river Annan. At Lockerbie we
leave the main line of railway, and diverge by a branch westwards to Dumfries, passing the ruins of Lochmaben Castle,
which contests with Turnberry the honour of having been
the birthplace of Robert the Bruce. Soon after we reach

DUMFRIES,

the county town, and of ancient date, having become a royal
burgh so early as the 12th century. About seventy years thereafter, Devorgilla, daughter of Alan, last lord of Galloway, and
mother of John Baliol, erected a monastery here for Franciscan
friars, in the church of which Robert the Bruce slew the Red
Comyn before the high altar. About the same time she built a
bridge across the Nith, and the pontage was given as an endow-
ment to the same religious foundation. This remarkable
structure consisted originally of thirteen arches, with a barrier
in the centre ; but they have been reduced to six, and the bridge
is now only crossed by foot-passengers.

It was in Dumfries that the poet Burns passed the closing
years of his life, and the modest mansion in which he died may
still be seen. He was buried in the old churchyard of St.

Michael's Church, where a monument has been erected to his
memory.

The environs of Dumfries include several beautiful country
seats, among which are LINCLUDEN HOUSE (near the ruins of
Lincluden Abbey) and Dalswinton House. When Burns
visited Edinburgh, on the publication of a second edition of
his poems, he became acquainted with Mr. Patrick Millar (at
that time the proprietor of Dalswinton); and it was on his
invitation that he entered as tenant on the farm of Ellisland, then a portion of the Dalswinton estate, but dissevered a
number of years ago. At Ellisland he produced his famous
poem of "Tam o' Shanter," and the pathetic ode to "Mary in
Heaven." Here his son, Colonel William Burns, was born.

At a short distance from the adjacent wooden railway bridge
is the mansion-house of Friars' Carse, where the "Ayrshire
ploughman" was frequently an honoured guest. His kind
and amiable friend, Major Riddell, dispensed here a generous
hospitality, and at his table the well-known contest for "the
whistle" took place in the old Scandinavian fashion. On one
of the windows of the rustic fog-house Burns inscribed verses
containing the familiar lines :—

> "Life is but a day at most,
> Sprung from night, in darkness lost."

Near Closeburn station (11¾ miles from Dumfries) is Closeburn
Hall (F. Villiers, Esq.), an ancient seat of the Kirkpatricks, one of
whom was the associate of Robert Bruce in the slaughter of
Comyn, and from whom the ex-Empress of France is descended
in the maternal line. In its vicinity is the romantic dell called
Crickhope Linn. The station next to Closeburn is Thornhill,
2½ miles to the westward of which is Drumlanrig Castle, the
Dumfriesshire seat of the Duke of Buccleuch and Queensberry.
The castle was built by William, first Duke of Queensberry,
who is said to have slept only one night within its walls,
and it continued to be the principal residence of the Queensberry family, until it passed by right of entail into the family of
the present proprietor in 1810. It was much defaced by the
Highland rebels who occupied it in 1745, and a portrait of
William III., by Godfrey Kneller, still bears the marks of
their violence. The castle is open to the view of the public
on Tuesdays and Fridays, and the gardens are well worthy of a

visit. The park is of great extent and beauty, and is intersected by the river Nith.

𝔑𝔢𝔴 or 𝔖𝔴𝔢𝔢𝔱𝔥𝔢𝔞𝔯𝔱 𝔄𝔟𝔟𝔢𝔶, a beautiful remnant of Gothic architecture, lies eight miles to the south of Dumfries, on the opposite coast of Kirkcudbrightshire, and near the base of Criffel. The tower is light and airy, and tolerably entire. The predominating style is the Early English, in its best day, but the windows have had the advantage of the Second Pointed or Decorated style. The Abbey was erected in 1275 by Devorgilla, as a tribute of affection to the memory of John Baliol, her husband, whose death occurred six years previously. Immediately to the south is the conical-peaked Criffel, which rises to the height of 1867 feet, and commands one of the most extensive views in the south of Scotland.

Another interesting ruin near Dumfries is Caerlaverock Castle, situated nine miles to the south of the town, on the north shore of the Solway Firth, betwixt the confluence of the rivers Nith and Lochar. For a long period this castle was the chief seat of the Maxwells, Earls of Nithsdale ; and the property on which it stands still belongs to Lord Herries, the representative of that ancient family. · The castle was at one time a place of great strength, and with a garrison of only 60 men it resisted for a considerable time a powerful army led by Edward I. It is triangular, and surrounded by a wet ditch. Of the towers which originally stood at each angle, the only one remaining is Murdoch's, where Murdoch, Duke of Albany, was confined in the year 1425. Over the entrance-gate to the courtyard is the crest of the Maxwells, with the date of the last repairs, and the motto, "I bid ye fair."

In the old churchyard of Caerlaverock a headstone has been "erected to the memory of Robert Paterson, the Old Mortality of Sir Walter Scott, who was buried here February 1801."

A short and pleasant excursion may be made to Terregles and Irongray. At the former, 3 miles from Dumfries, Queen Mary spent a few hours before her ill-fated flight to England, and various relics of that visit are still preserved in Terregles House. Terregles was the residence of the Earls of Nithsdale, and is now possessed by the Hon. M. C. Maxwell. Irongray Churchyard, 2 miles beyond Terregles, contains a tombstone erected by the author of "Waverley" to the memory of Helen Walker (the Jeanie Deans of the "Heart of Midlothian.")

DUMFRIES TO STRANRAER AND PORTPATRICK.

[By railway through Kirkcudbright and Wigton shires.]

This route affords the tourist an opportunity of viewing the extreme southern coast of Scotland. Leaving Dumfries, we proceed by Dalbeattie, a thriving place, near which is the old castle of Buittle, and 4 miles farther reach Castle Douglas— a neat and well-built town. In its vicinity is Carlingwark Loch, covering a surface of 100 acres, and studded with picturesque little islands. On a small island in the Dee, about a mile to the west, is Threave Castle, an old stronghold of the Douglases. A short distance to the south is Gelston Castle, a modern building, erected by the late Sir William Douglas.

In the neighbourhood of Creetown are several valuable granite quarries, from which the new Liverpool docks were built. In the manse of this parish, Dr. Thomas Brown, the distinguished philosopher, was born in 1778; and he was buried in the old churchyard. The scene of a part of the novel of "Guy Mannering" is laid in this neighbourhood, and Dirk Hatteraick's cave is pointed out on the coast between Creetown and Gatehouse.

Kirkcudbright, the capital of the county, is situated 6 miles below the confluence of the Dee with the Tarff, these rivers here forming an estuary called Kirkcudbright Bay. A branch railway connects it with Castle-Douglas, from which it is distant about 11 miles. It is surrounded with terraced woods and romantic walks, and connected with the Borgue side of the Dee by a handsome metal bridge. The modern parish church is a conspicuous object, contrasting with the ivy-covered ruins of the old castle of the Maclellans. St. Mary's Isle, the seat of the Earl of Selkirk, is situated on a beautifully-wooded peninsula, a mile and a half to the south of the town. Six miles to the south-east is Dundrennan Abbey, founded A.D. 1142, having an interesting connection with Queen Mary, who fled hither after her defeat at Langside. The portion of the abbey now standing has been thoroughly repaired by the Commissioners of Woods and Forests. There is a small inn at the village, where refreshments may be obtained. About 8 miles westwards are Gatehouse-of-Fleet, and Cally House, the seat of Murray Stewart, Esq.

Fourteen miles north-west of Castle-Douglas is the town of
New Galloway, situated nearly in the centre of Kirkcudbrightshire, at the northern extremity of Loch Ken. This lake is
formed by the river Ken, and is about 10 miles in length and
half-a-mile in breadth; it is fringed with wood and surrounded
by mountains. In the vicinity is Kenmure Castle, a place
of considerable antiquity, with an avenue of fine old lime-
trees.

We enter Wigtownshire at NEWTON-STEWART—a neat town,
with some 2500 inhabitants, situated on the banks of the river
Cree, which is here spanned by a handsome bridge of five
arches. An excursion may be made from this to Loch Trool, a
beautiful little lake, about 14 miles distant. The lake is
about 2 miles long, fringed with wood, and surrounded by
mountains, some of which rise to between 2000 and 3000 feet
high.

Six miles to the south of Newton-Stewart, on a slight eminence, is WIGTOWN, the capital of the county, with a population
of about 2000. Many of the houses are elegantly built, and the
principal street is so wide as to admit of a large bowling-green
in its centre. The parish church is modern. In the old churchyard there is an interesting memorial of the two female martyrs
who were drowned in the Bladenoch in the year 1685; and on
the height above a monument has been erected to their memory.
To the south is Galloway House, the principal seat of the Earl
of Galloway, situated at the seaport of Garlieston. Of the
cathedral church of Galloway, built about the end of the 12th
century, little remains except a ruined and roofless chancel,
occupying the site of much more ancient buildings, which had
been the crypt, as it would seem, of an extensive church. It is
a well-proportioned and beautiful specimen of the Early English
style, and within the last forty years has been used as the parish
church. The western doorway is in fine preservation and
worthy of a careful examination. The town of Glenluce is situated about a mile and a half from the most inland point of
Luce Bay. A little to the west of the town are the ruins of
Glenluce Abbey, founded A.D. 1190 by Alan, Lord of Galloway.
The original buildings must have been extensive, but the
chapter-house is the only portion in fair preservation.

The only other town of importance in Wigtownshire is

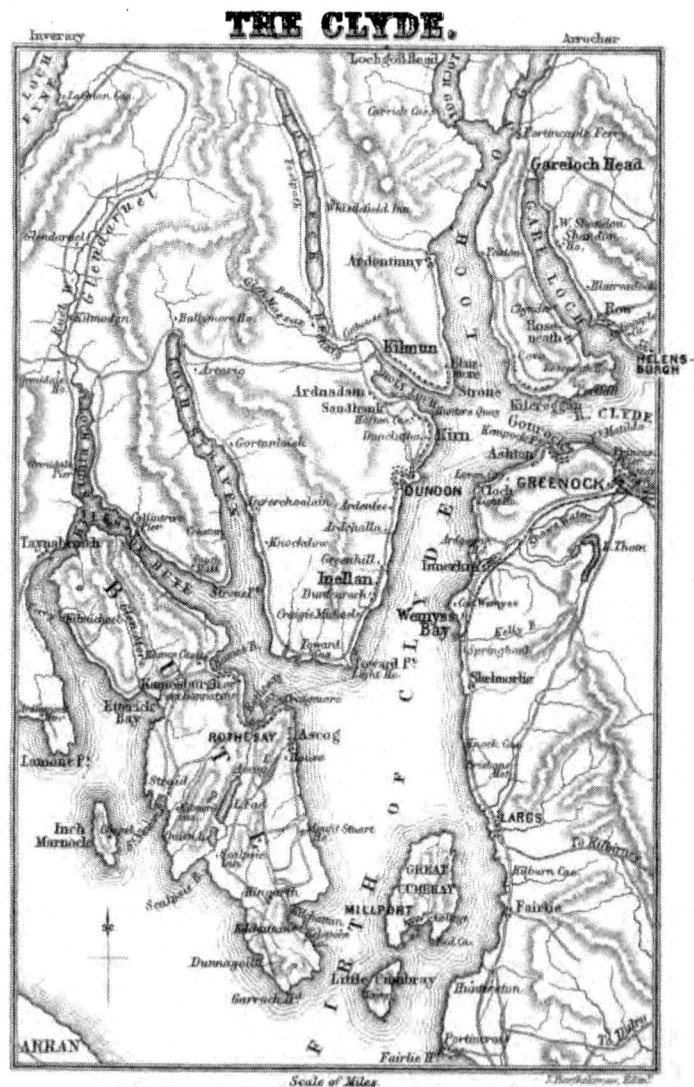

THE CLYDE.

Scale of Miles

A.& C. Black Edinburgh.

STRANRAER,

a seaport, situated at the head of Loch Ryan. It contains no antiquities, but there are several gentlemen's seats in the neighbourhood, the principal of which are—Loch Insh (Earl of Stair), Lochnaw Castle (Sir Andrew Agnew, Bart.), Dunskey (Col. Blair). In the neighbourhood, about 4 miles distant, are the ruins of Castle Kennedy, formerly the seat of the powerful Earls of Cassilis, who for 300 years took a leading part in Galloway affairs. It is now the property of the Earl of Stair.

At a short distance to the south, situated on a peninsula jutting out into a small lake, are the remains of Soulseat, the most ancient monastery in Galloway.

Seven miles and a half to the west of Stranraer is PORT-PATRICK, with an extensive harbour, on which large sums of money have been expended. Portpatrick is the nearest point to the Irish coast, being distant only 21½ miles.

GLASGOW TO DUMBARTON AND GREENOCK.

By the River Clyde.

Starting from the Broomielaw in one of the numerous steamers* which ply on the coast, a few minutes' sail brings us to the villages of Govan and Partick, where several of the extensive shipbuilding-yards of the Clyde are situated.

In about an hour's sail we reach BOWLING ; a short distance below which is Dunglas Point, where a monument has been erected to the memory of Henry Bell, who first introduced steam-navigation on the Clyde. The Wall of Antoninus, or Graham's Dyke, is supposed to have had its western termination here.

A little beyond this we reach

DUMBARTON CASTLE,

situated on a rock which rises to the height of 240 feet. A part of the castle bears the name of " Wallace's Tower," in comme-

* By taking the railway to Greenock, in order to catch the steamer there, the tourist may leave Glasgow about an hour later (see Time Tables).

moration of the Scottish hero, who was confined here; and a
huge two-handed sword, said to have been his, is still shown.
During the wars which desolated Scotland in the reign of Queen
Mary, this fortress was taken, by a clever stratagem, by Captain Crawford of Jordanhill, a distinguished adherent of the
king's party.   At the back of the rock may be seen the town of
Dumbarton, a place of great industry, where shipbuilding is
carried on to a great extent.

At a short distance from Dumbarton formerly stood the castle
of Cardross, in which King Robert Bruce died.   We next pass
Newark Castle, a large quadrangular building, and Port-Glasgow,
shortly thereafter arriving at

GREENOCK,

[Hotels: Tontine; White Hart; Royal.]

a seaport ranking as one of the most considerable in Great
Britain, though of comparatively modern origin.   It contains
several most elegant harbours, occupying an extent of many
acres, with accompanying piers, and a fine esplanade built along
the sea-shore.   The principal trades carried on are the refining
of sugar and shipbuilding.   The latter, especially the construction of iron steam-vessels, is of great extent.

The situation of Greenock is at once beautiful and convenient
for commerce.   The view seawards embraces the mountains of
Argyleshire and Dumbartonshire, and the openings to the various
sea-lochs that indent the opposite coast, including the Gareloch
and Loch Long.   Close upon the steamboat quay stands the
Custom-house, and in Cathcart Street are the Court-house,
several churches, banks, a theatre, and a club-house.   In the
burying-ground of the Old West Kirk of Greenock Burns's
"Highland Mary" is interred.   In Union Street (west end of
the town) is the Watt Institute, erected by a son of the great
engineer, containing a Public Library, and a portrait of John
Galt the novelist, who died in Greenock.   The cemetery of
Greenock is one of the finest in the kingdom; and there are
two public parks, the gifts of Sir Michael Shaw-Stewart, Bart.,
lord of the manor.   An extensive sandbank, called the Tail
of the Bank, terminates a little below Greenock, and is considered the best anchorage in the Firth of Clyde.

The following steamboat excursions may conveniently be made from Greenock :—

1. To Loch Long and Arrochar, *via* Dunoon, Blairmore, and Ardentinny. At Arrochar time is given to those returning to Greenock or other piers to cross to Tarbet on Loch Lomond, and view that beautiful lake ; or the tourist may proceed from Arrochar to Inverary by coach, which runs, in connection with the steamer, *via* Glencroe and Rest-and-be-Thankful.

2. To Loch Goil (a branch of Loch Long) and Lochgoilhead, from which coaches also run to Inverary, *via* Hell's Glen and St. Catherine's Ferry.

3. To Helensburgh, the Gareloch, and Garelochhead, by Roseneath.

4. To Kilmun and the Holy Loch, crossing the mouth of Loch Long.

5. To Largs, Millport, and Arran.

6. To Inverary by the " Lord of the Isles " Steamer.

Assuming that the tourist adopts one or other of these routes leading to Inverary, he will be conducted through some of the finest loch and mountain scenery to the capital of Argyleshire,

· INVERARY,

[*Hotels:* The Argyll Arms ; The George.]

the county town, situated near the head of Loch Fyne, where the river Aray falls into the loch. It was erected into a royal burgh in 1648 by Charles I. while a prisoner in Carisbrook Castle, and has been for a long period the seat of the noble family of Argyll. The town consists mainly of one street, near the centre of which stands the church. Here a monument has been erected to several members of the clan Campbell who were massacred near the spot in 1685. The ancient market-cross is a fine example of the sculptured stones peculiar to Scotland,

Inverary Castle, the seat of the Duke of Argyll, was built on the site of the old castle by Duke Archibald, in 1748, after a plan by Adam. It is a square building, constructed of chlorite-slate, flanked with round towers, and surmounted with a square winged pavilion. It contains a spacious hall, and the drawing-room is adorned with some fine tapestry. There are numerous family portraits, including those of the great Marquis of Argyll and his son, who were both beheaded.

Duniquoich Hill, a cone-shaped hill, 700 feet high, overlooks

the town and castle, and is an excellent point from which to
obtain a view.

Inverary is an important herring-fishery station, and the fish
caught here are celebrated for their quality.

From Inverary a very pleasant tour may be made by coach to
Loch Awe and Oban. The first portion of this road is carried
through Glenaray. Afterwards it descends upon the beautiful
expanse of

LOCH AWE.

This loch is about 30 miles in length, and from 1 to 2 in breadth.
It is reckoned one of the most picturesque in the Highlands;
and possesses some pretty islands. Among these are Inishail,
on which are the ruins of a small chapel; Inis-Eraith, the scene
of one of Ossian's tales; Innis-Chonnel, on which are the ruins of
an ancient castle, a former seat of the Argyll family; and Fraoch-
Elain, containing the ruins of a castle, once the property of the
chief of the clan M'Naughton. At the southern extremity of
the loch is Ford (see page 113), from whence there is coach communication with Ardrishaig. A small but comfortable screw
steamer plies up and down the loch once a day, affording an
opportunity of viewing the scenery on all sides. At Port Sona-
chan ¦there is a ferry, where a road strikes off to Taynuilt.
The point of land jutting into the lake near Cladich is named
Innistrynich, or the Island of the Druids.

The chapel on the islet of Inishail was suppressed at the
Reformation, and its possessions erected into a temporary lordship in favour of Hay, abbot of Inchaffray, who abjured the
Roman Catholic faith. The old churchyard contains a number
of ancient tombstones, curiously carved, many of them bearing
the name of the ancient clan "MacArthur," the original inhabitants of these shores.

On a peninsula at the head of the loch stand the ruins of
KILCHURN CASTLE, founded in 1449 by the lady of Sir Colin
Campbell, while her husband, the Black Knight of Rhodes,
was engaged in the wars of the crusades. This chieftain, who
was second son of Sir Duncan Campbell of Lochawe, and
ancestor of the Argyll family, acquired by marriage a considerable portion of the estates of the family of Lorn, and was the
founder of the powerful family of Breadalbane. So late as 1745

Kilchurn was garrisoned by the Royal troops, and the exterior and greater part of the interior walls are still entire. A few miles inland from Kilchurn is the village of Dalmally, situated at the mouth of Glen Orchy. It contains a good hotel.

Two miles northwards of Dalmally is Glenstrae. This, with the neighbouring glen, formed a district peopled by the Clan Gregor, whose expatriation forms the lament in Scott's gathering song of the clan :—

> " Glenorchy's proud mountains, Coalchuirn and her towers,
> Glenstrae, and Glenlyon, no longer are ours ;
> We're landless, landless, Gregalich !"

"It's a far cry to Lochow" was the slogan of the clan, indicating the impossibility of reaching them in these remote fastnesses.

The head of the loch is crossed by the Callander and Oban Railway, which supplies an agreeable facility for the continuation of this route. It is carried through the famous pass of Awe, where the river Awe is disgorged from the lake. This pass is about 3 miles in length, and terminates on the west at the Rock of Brander. In this defile the Clan M'Dougall of Lorn was nearly destroyed by King Robert Bruce. The river is crossed by the "*Bridge of Awe,*" the scene of Sir Walter Scott's tale of "The Highland Widow." This is about the best point from which to ascend Ben Cruachan, a mountain remarkable for its noble proportions. It has two peaks, the highest of which is 3667 feet above the sea-level.

Two and a half miles onwards is Taynuilt Hotel, beyond which the road skirts the borders of Loch Etive, one of the most beautiful sea-lochs in the Highlands. On the north side are seen Ardchattan House and the ruins of a priory. At the entrance of the loch are Connell Ferry and Hotel, and 2 miles beyond the ruins of Dunstaffnage Castle. Soon after passing these we arrive at Oban, which is described in a subsequent page (114).

LOCH LONG AND LOCH GOIL.

[Regular steamers from Greenock ply up and down both lochs.]

Loch Long is an extended arm of the sea that strikes off from the Firth of Clyde opposite Gourock. It is 24 miles in length, with an average breadth of a mile. It stretches first in a northerly and afterwards in a north-easterly direction, separating the counties of Dumbarton and Argyle. About half-way up

Loch Long, Loch Goil branches off to the north-west. Both
lochs are famed for the romantic character of their scenery.
The mouth of Loch Long is studded with clusters of villas,
named respectively Kilcreggan, Cove, and Blairmore. Half-
way between Blairmore and the mouth of Loch Goil is Ardentinny, where a road strikes across the hills, *via* Loch Eck, to
Strachur on Loch Fyne side, where there is a ferry to Inverary.
At the head of Loch Goil is the village of Lochgoilhead, and at
the head of Loch Long that of Arrochar, at both of which there
are hotels. The routes from these places have been already
referred to.

LARGS, MILLPORT, AND ARRAN.

[Arran may be reached from Glasgow either *via* Ardrossan or Wemyss Bay,
and thence per steamer; or all the way by steamer from Greenock,
calling at Largs and Millport.

N.B.—As the hours of sailing are liable to change, it is advisable to consult
the Glasgow newspaper of the day before starting.]

The Wemyss Bay Railway is a single line about 10 miles
in length, branching off from the Caledonian Railway at
Upper Greenock. Thence it proceeds by the village of Inver-
kip, near which stands Ardgowan House (Sir Michael Shaw-
Stewart, Bart.,) to Wemyss Bay. The terminus is connected
with a pier, where the steamer awaits the arrival of passengers.
There are some elegant villas at Wemyss Bay, including Castle
Wemyss (John Burns, Esq.) Going on board here, a pleasant
sail along the Ayrshire coast, past the modern watering-place of
Skelmorlie, brings us to

LARGS,

an ancient town built on a level piece of ground, where the
battle of Largs, between the Scots and Haco, king of Norway,
was fought in 1263. The town is surrounded by numerous fine
villas, and commands a view of the Cumbrae island and peaks of
Arran. In the vicinity is Kelburn Castle, a seat of the Earl of
Glasgow. From Largs the steamer crosses to the town of

MILLPORT,

which lies snugly on the margin of a deep bay on the south
coast of the Great Cumbrae Island; two small islands, called
the Arrans, afford excellent shelter to the pier and harbour,
which have both been constructed by the Marquis of

Bute. The island is 3½ miles long by 2 broad, and is the joint property of the Earl of Glasgow and Marquis of Bute. The Episcopal College erected here is an elegant building, and there are numerous well-built houses and villas. The Little Cumbrae Island lies one mile and a half to the south. From Millport we cross the mouth of the Firth of Clyde to the

ISLAND OF ARRAN.

The steamer on approaching the shore passes the mouth of Glen Sannox, and shortly after calls at the small port of CORRIE, where there is a good inn. It then proceeds to Brodick Bay, where there is a large hotel, close to the new iron pier. From Brodick Bay, the elegant shape of Goatfell is seen to great advantage, rising above the battlements of Brodick Castle, the residence of the Duke of Hamilton, to whom nearly the whole island belongs. GOATFELL is 2875 feet above the level of the sea, and is easily ascended in from four to five hours.

An excursion is frequently made to Loch Ranza, situated on the north side of the island, about 12 miles from Brodick. Upon a small peninsula near the entrance are the ruins of an old castle, which was once a royal hunting seat.

On leaving Brodick Bay the steamer sails round Clachland Point to the village of Lamlash, which is built on the edge of a bay of the same name. This bay is sheltered by the Holy Island, an irregular cone, 900 feet high. Here St. Molios, a disciple of St. Columba, is said to have founded a church, and the cave in which he resided is still pointed out.

At the southerly point of Lamlash Bay (three miles from the village) a simple unhewn monolith marks the point whence Robert Bruce embarked for the coast of Carrick. Specimens of rude sepulchral pillars, cairns, and circles, are to be found in various parts of the island.

To the geologist and botanist the island presents very interesting features. The shores are, for the most part, formed of red sandstone. The next most conspicuous rocks are of a schistose nature, and of various composition. The soil gives birth to a varied system of vegetation. Thus we have plants of the sea-shore, secluded glen, open morass, and bleak mountain-top, within the compass of a few miles. In cryptogamic plants Arran is peculiarly rich.

CLYDE STEAMER ROUTE.

GREENOCK TO OBAN.

This route, which may be commenced either at Glasgow or (by taking the rail) at Greenock, forms on the whole the most agreeable mode of approach to the Western Highlands of Scotland.

On leaving Greenock, where the passengers who have come from Glasgow by train are received, the steamer crosses the estuary of the Clyde and approaches the Cowal district of Argyleshire, on which stands Dunoon, with its numerous villas, and two piers, at the more easterly of which, named *Kirn*, it makes its first call. On a conical hill, rising close above the main pier, stand the ruins of Dunoon Castle, of which the Duke of Argyll is the hereditary keeper. A few miles from Dunoon is the Holy Loch, a beautiful inlet of the sea, on which are situated the villages of Hunter's Quay, Ardenadam, Kilmun, and Strone. At Kilmun the Argyll family have their burial-place.

Leaving Dunoon, the steamer skirts the shore of the Bullwood, and shortly after reaches Inellan, the houses of which form almost a continuation of Dunoon. The peninsula of Cowal terminates a few miles lower, at Toward Point, where there is a lighthouse. A little farther we come in sight of Toward Castle (A. S. Finlay, Esq.), and, crossing the channel, arrive at

ROTHESAY,

the county town of Bute, situated at the head of a well-formed bay. It contains several hotels and a hydropathic establishment. In the centre of the town are the ruins of Rothesay Castle, once a royal residence, and supposed to have been built about the year 1100. Robert II. created his eldest son Duke of Rothesay, a title still borne by the Prince of Wales. The castle was burned by a brother of the Earl of Argyll in 1685, and has since lain in ruins; but the present Marquis of Bute has cleared away the rubbish with which the ruins were encumbered, and surrounded them by a railing. Adjoining the parish church, situated about half-a-mile southwards, are the ruins of the old kirk of St. Mary's, containing several interesting stone effigies, and the burial-vault of the Bute family. Mount Stuart, the family mansion of the Marquis of Bute, is 5 miles from Rothesay, on the east side of the island.

The climate of Bute is so mild that it has been compared to that of Devonshire.

After leaving Rothesay, we enter THE KYLES OF BUTE, a sound or strait separating the northern part of Bute from the coast of Cowal. Passing the mouth of Loch Striven we reach the pier of Colintraive, situated near the mouth of Loch Ridden. Here the channel is contracted by four small islands, one of which contains the ruins of a fort erected by the Earl of Argyll in 1685. Near the head of Loch Ridden are Ormidale (Mrs. Campbell) and Glendaruel House (Archibald Campbell, Esq.) At the entrance on the west side is Glen Caladh (G. R. Stephenson, Esq.) The Kyles terminate a little beyond Tignabruich, at Ardlamont Point, where we enter Loch Fyne, a view being afforded on the south of the hills of Arran and the peninsula of Cantire.

This peninsula is joined to South Knapdale by a narrow isthmus at the fishing village of Tarbert, where a temporary pier has been constructed outside the loch for the use of the steamer on this route. The ruins of an old castle, built by Robert Bruce in 1326, overlook the harbour. From Tarbert a coach runs during summer to Campbeltown, the chief town, situated in a bay near the southern extremity of Cantire. It is well built, and contains a beautifully sculptured market-cross.

Proceeding up Loch Fyne, we diverge into Lochgilp, which branches off on the west at the point where Loch Fyne becomes contracted. Here is situated the village of

ARDRISHAIG.*

[Hotel: Ardrishaig. 2 miles from Lochgilphead, 11¼ from Tarbert, 26¼ from Inverary, 49 from Campbeltown.]

the south-eastern terminus of the Crinan Canal, and where there is a good pier and harbour for fishing boats. The more important village of Lochgilphead stands at the head of the sea-arm, and on the opposite side of the bay is Kilmory Castle (Sir John

* During summer a coach runs in connection with the steamers from Ardrishaig to Ford on Loch Awe, where a steam-gondola conveys passengers to Brander, at the head of the Loch. Here passengers can join the Callander and Oban Railway route. The road, between Ardrishaig and Ford, passes the village of Kilmartin, famous for its sculptured stones. The sail up Loch Awe from Ford is beautiful but tedious. (See page 108.)

I

P. Orde, Bart.) About 10 miles from Lochgilphead, on Loch
Fyne side, is Minard Castle, the seat of J. Pender, Esq., M.P.
The Crinan Canal, which commences here, was formed to avoid
the circuitous passage round the Mull of Cantire. It is 9 miles
in length, with fifteen locks. The boats are comfortably fitted
up and drawn by steam. After going on board we pass, on
the left, Auchindarroch House, and the Bishop of Argyll's
chapel and palace, and farther on Carnbaan Inn, a good station
for anglers. Along the whole course of the canal there stretches
an extensive plain, on the rising ground to the right of which is
Poltalloch House (John Malcolm, Esq., M.P.) Before reaching
Crinan, we may observe the old village of Crinan, built upon a
picturesque rock, which becomes an island at high water.
Beyond is seen Duntroon Castle. The modern village of Crinan
forms the north-western terminus of the canal. Upon the right,
on the opposite side of the bay, is the castle of Duntroon ; and
northward, on the same side, is Loch Craignish, an arm of the
sea, intersected by a chain of islands.

The sail from Crinan to Oban occupies 2¼ hours. The steamboat proceeds through the Dorishtmore or Great Gate, at the
point of Craignish, then through the Sound of Scarba, stopping
generally at the islet of Easdale, where there are slate-quarries.
The steamer keeps close to the shore, passing on the left a small
island called Innishcapel.

On arriving at Kerrara Island, the mountains of Mull appear
to great advantage, the highest of which is Benmore (3185).
Loch Feochan opens on the right, disclosing Ben Cruachan to
view. On approaching nearer, the ruins of Gylen Castle, an old
stronghold of the Macleans of Duart, rise on the left, while on
the right is passed the house of Macdougall of Galanach. The
island of Kerrara forms a natural breakwater to the bay of Oban.

OBAN.

[*Hotels :* The Great Western ; Alexandra ; Caledonian ; King's Arms ;
Imperial ; Queen's ;—Craig-Ard, and Grand, on hill above.]

This town, which is a great rendezvous for tourists in the
West Highlands, is built along the margin of the bay just referred to. Being of comparatively modern origin the houses are
well built, and it contains excellent shops and very good hotel
accommodation.

On a rocky promontory, about half-a-mile distant from the town, are the ruins of Dunolly Castle, access to which is granted on certain days. Three miles to the north, at the union of Loch Etive with Loch Linnhe, stand the ruins of *Dunstaffnage Castle,* said to have been the seat of the Scottish monarchy until the overthrow of the Picts, when that honour was transferred to Scone. It is still the property of the Crown. It was here that the famous Stone of Destiny was deposited, which now forms the support of the coronation-chair in Westminster Abbey.

STAFFA AND IONA.

These interesting islands may be visited by regular steamers from Oban on each day of the week. In fine weather the sail occupies eleven hours, allowing an hour at Staffa and another at Iona. Passengers are landed at both places in small boats belonging to the steamers. In rough weather the landing is on the north-east side of Staffa, involving a walk of three quarters of a mile to the entrance of Fingal's Cave.

The steamer proceeds through the Sound of Mull, calling at the village of Tobermory. Beyond this it passes, on the right, the entrance to Loch Sunart, and on the left *Bloody Bay,* the scene of a clan battle. To the west of Ardmore Point stands the castle of Mingarry, anciently a residence of the clan Macdonald.

THE ISLAND OF STAFFA

is about 8 miles distant from the western coast of Mull. It is of an irregularly oval shape, about a mile and a half in circumference, and is about 144 feet in height at its highest point. It is covered with luxuriant grass, and affords good pasture for cattle. In calm weather passengers are conveyed from the steamer in small boats into Fingal's Cave, which is accessible at all states of the tide except that of extreme high water.

The cave is nearly 70 feet in height, and recedes about 230 feet. The entire front, as well as the sides, is composed of ranges of columns, beautifully jointed, and of most symmetrical forms ; and the roof exhibits a rich grouping of overhanging pillars.

The other caves are the Clam or Scallop-shell Cave and the Herdsman. In the former the basaltic columns are bent like the ribs of a ship. From Buachaille, or the Herdsman—a conoidal pile of columns about 30 feet high—the pillars extend along the whole face of the cliff to the entrance of Fingal's Cave.

Iona

or Icolmkill is a small island, about 9 miles to the south of Staffa. It is nearly 3 miles in length and 1 in breadth, containing about 500 inhabitants. It is celebrated as an early seat of Christianity, and as the spot where Saint Columba, an Irish Christian missionary, took up his abode in the year 563.*

The stranger is generally conducted first to the *Nunnery* of St. Mary, which is in comparatively good preservation. Among the tombs may be seen that of the Prioress Anna, of date 1511. From this we proceed along the *street of the dead* to *Reilig Oran*, the burial-ground of Iona, passing on the way one of those Runic crosses for which this island is famous, named Maclean's Cross. The tombs of this cemetery are disposed in nine rows, one being appropriated by the Macleans, another by the Macdonalds, while a third is pointed out as the spot where

"The mighty kings of three fair realms are laid."

As a specimen of Celtic art, the finest tomb is the memorial slab of the four Friars, which occurs in the fifth row.

We next visit *St. Oran's Chapel*, which appears to have been erected about the close of the 11th century by Margaret, Queen of Malcolm Canmore, on the site of St. Columba's original cell. It is of small extent (40 by 20), and of rude Norman architecture, and contains some interesting monuments.

The Cathedral.

Before entering the Cathedral Church of St. Mary we should examine the beautiful St. Martin's Cross, which is considered a model of handsome proportions. It is formed of one piece of red granite, 14 feet high, and is covered with Runic sculpture. The Cathedral is built in the usual form of a cross; the length being 160 feet and the breadth 24. It consists of nave, tran-

* For an interesting account of St. Columba and his adopted home, see the work on Iona by the Duke of Argyll, who is proprietor of the island.

septs, and choir, at the north side of which is a sacristy, and
there are side chapels on the south.　It is chiefly in the First
Pointed style of architecture; but, as in other buildings of the
same kind in Scotland, there is a mixture of the Romanesque
and Second Pointed styles, indicating different periods of erection, ranging from the 13th to the 16th centuries.　The tower,
which is divided into three storeys, is supported by four arches,
resting on thick-set pillars, with sculptured capitals.　Very near
the place where the high altar stood is a black marble tombstone of Abbot Mackinnon, whose cross is in St. Oran's Chapel;
and opposite is one of Abbot Kenneth.　In the centre of the
chancel is the tomb of Macleod of Macleod, the largest tombstone in Iona.　On the north of the Cathedral are the ruins of
the cloisters, consisting of a chapter-house and library.

"Strangers visiting Iona," says the Duke of Argyll, in his
interesting work already referred to, "who have time to do so,
should take a boat from the landing-place to the Port-na-
Churaich, the creek where Columba landed.　The beach consists of fragments of rocks rolled and polished by the surf, and
is almost like a beach of precious stones."

BALLACHULISH AND GLENCOE.

During the summer months a steamer sails from Oban, on
each day of the week except Sunday, to Ballachulish, where
vehicles are in waiting to convey passengers to Glencoe.　After
viewing the glen they are reconveyed to the hotel or to the
steamer, which returns that evening to Oban.　The route pur-
sued is the same as to Inverness, *via* the Caledonian Canal as
far as Ballachulish.

SKYE.

This island may now be reached either by steamer from Oban,
sailing on certain days of the week, or by railway from Dingwall to Strome, thence by steamer to Portree.

Skye is one of the most considerable islands of the Hebrides,
and belongs to the county of Inverness.　Its greatest length is 54
miles, and breadth 33, varying, however, to so little as 3 miles;
and it contains some 700 square miles.　It is separated from the
mainland of Scotland by the sounds of Sleat and Raasay, but at

the ferry of Glenelg it is not more than half-a-mile from the nearest part of Inverness-shire. The coasts are bold and rocky, abounding with many safe and commodious bays, especially at the harbours of Oronsay and Portree. It is celebrated for the picturesque grandeur of its mountains, some of which are so high as to be snow-capped at midsummer. The only town in the island is Portree.

Supposing the tourist to visit the island by steamer from Oban, he may disembark either at Kyle Akin or Broadford, and proceed thence, by Lochs Scavaig and Coruisk, to Sligachan and Portree.

If this route be chosen, we reach, at the distance of 5 miles from Broadford, a small cluster of huts at the head of Loch Slapin called Torrin, where, during the summer months, boats may be hired for the next part of the excursion. This consists of the sail from Torrin to the head of Loch Scavaig, a distance of about 10 miles, and which, by means of stout rowers, may be accomplished in about two hours. On the right will be observed Mount Blaven, 3019 feet in height. Passing the farm-house of Kilmaree, and coasting along the island, we reach the

SPAR CAVE OF STRATHAIRD,

the entrance to which is rather unpromising. An advance of a few yards from the opening unfolds the interior, which recedes some 160 feet into the solid rock, and seems as if paved with marble. The floor forms a steep incline, and is so smooth as to be ascended with difficulty, especially as it is necessary to carry a lighted candle in one hand. The innermost recess opens into a gallery, with crystallisations, and the cave terminates at the brink of a deep pool, 10 feet in diameter.

Leaving the cave and rounding Strathaird Point, with the island of Soa on the left, we enter

LOCH SCAVAIG,

bounded by the romantic forms of the Cuchullin Hills. The rocky coast is here broken up by the action of the sea into caverns, one of which, passed on the right, is said to have been inhabited by Prince Charles shortly before his final departure for France. At the foot of Blaven, to the right, is Camasunary, where ponies may be engaged to be in waiting. The upper portion of Loch Scavaig is divided into two smaller basins, and it is from the westerly one we proceed to *Loch Coruisk*, which is distant only a mile from the landing-place. The margins of this lake are composed of sloping rocks and gigantic stones, rising ridge above ridge till they blend with the higher sides of the mountains. The whole scene is one of sterile grandeur. The tourist may strike across from Loch Coruisk to Glen Sligachan, by skirting the ridge called Drumhain.

Of the numerous peaks of the Cuchullins which here come into view, Scuir-na-Gillean (the Rock of the Young Men) is generally regarded as the highest. Its height is computed to be between 3200 and 3220 feet. Descending into Glen Sligachan, the small Loch-na-nain will be seen, where the road from Camasunary is met. The road through this desolate valley is rough and stony, and although said to be only 4½ miles it will appear to many at least double in point of fatigue. Following the course of the rivulet, we reach

SLIGACHAN HOTEL,

situated about ten minutes' walk from the head of the sea loch of that name. Opposite the hotel rises Glamaig, and to the east Marscow, both extraordinary-looking peaks. The distance from Sligachan to Portree is 9½ miles, but the road presents no particular feature of interest.

PORTREE,

[*Hotels:* Portree; Royal; Caledonian. 25 miles from Broadford, 22 from Dunvegan.]

the chief town of Skye, is situated on a steep acclivity at the side of the loch of the same name, which here forms a landlocked natural harbour. The entrance is surrounded by bold headlands, forming the commencement of a noble range of coast scenery extending northward to the point of Aird. It derives its designation from James V., who anchored here for some time during an expedition to the Isles.

About five minutes' walk from the hotel is a rocky eminence surmounted by a tower, from which there is an extensive and beautiful prospect.

Five miles to the eastward of Portree lies the island of

Raasay, where Dr. Johnson and Boswell spent several days. Upon it are the hill of Duncan and the ruins of Brochel Castle.

On the coast, 4 miles northwards of Portree, is Prince Charles's Cave, where he lay concealed for some time during his wanderings.

Three miles distant from this, and 7 from Portree, is the remarkable mountain called

THE STORR ROCK,

the summit of which is cut down in a vertical face four or five hundred feet in height; while the steep declivity below is covered with huge masses of detached rock. The more durable remains of the cliffs are separated from the precipice, and combined in a variety of intricate groups, presenting forms of castles and towers. The most remarkable of all the rocks is that which forms the summit, and which is 160 feet in height from the ground (and 2341 above the level of the sea), and its form emulates at a distance the aspect of a spire. The prospect from the top of the Storr is very extensive, and embraces the greater part of Skye and other islands of the Hebrides, and the mountains of Ross and Sutherland.

THE QUIRAING

is another mountain in Skye, famous for its wonderful formation. It is situated about 20 miles to the north of Portree. In height it is inferior to the Storr, being only 1774 feet above the sea-level. That part which is more particularly entitled to the name of *Quiraing* consists of a verdant platform, about 1500 feet in height, 100 paces long by 60 broad. The passage by which it is approached is much obstructed by heaps of stones and rubbish, washed down or fallen during the waste of ages, while all around are gigantic columns of rock, for the most part inaccessible. One of these is an isolated pyramidal cliff, called the Needle. From Portree a visit may be paid to

DUNVEGAN CASTLE,

the residence of the Macleod of Macleod. It is situated on the shore of Loch Follart, in the district of Vaternish, very near the northern extremity of the island, 22 miles from Portree, and 25½ from Sligachan. There is very little to interest the tourist in either of the roads, and even the castle itself will hardly repay the time and trouble of visiting it.

STORNOWAY,

the only town of Lewis, and principal seaport, is situated at the
head of a bay on the east side of the island. It is a great fishing
station (taking precedence of all others save that of Wick), is
well and regularly built, and its streets are lighted with gas.
The most prominent of its buildings are the Parish Church,
Free Church, and Episcopal Chapel; the schools, jail, and
masonic lodge; it contains also a good inn. On an eminence
overlooking the town is the fine mansion of the proprietor, Sir
James Matheson, Bart., a building in the castellated Tudor
style. The castle grounds are extensive, and laid out with
great taste, and great improvements have been made in the property since it came into the possession of the present lord of the
manor, who has expended upwards of half-a-million on it in
various useful ways. The population of the island is now estimated at about 25,000.

The Druidical Standing-Stones or TEMPLE OF CALLANISH,
perhaps the most perfect remains of their kind in Britain,
may be visited from Stornoway.

Harris, the southern portion of this island, is much the
smaller of the two, and appended to Inverness-shire, whereas
Lewis forms part of Ross-shire. It is the property of the Earl
of Dunmore. At the head of Loch Seaforth is *Ardvourlie Castle*,
the shooting-lodge of E. H. Scott, Esq., and on west Loch
Tarbert, *Fincastle*, that of Earl de Grey.

At the southern point of the island are the remains of the
ancient church of Rowdill, containing an ancient monumental
tomb. The other islands of the Western Hebrides are Uist,
Benbecula, Barra, St. Kilda, and a number of smaller islands,
and the whole extend over a space of about 130 miles.

THE CALEDONIAN CANAL.

The Caledonian Canal consists of a chain of salt and fresh
water lakes, extending from the Atlantic to the German Ocean,
through what is called the Great Glen of Scotland, a distance of
60 miles. Of this, 37½ are natural sheets of water, and 23 cut
as canal. Taking our departure from Oban in one of the excellent steamers which sail on this route, we enter Loch Eil at

Coran Ferry, on a bend of which, near the confluence of the
river Lochy, stands

FORT-WILLIAM,

[*Hotels:* Alexandra ; The Chevalier ; The Caledonian.]

a small Highland town, which has sprung up in connection with
the adjacent fort. This fort was originally erected by General
Monk to overawe the untameable Sir Ewan Cameron of Loch
Eil, who persisted in waging war against the forces of the Commonwealth long after every other chieftain had recognised its
authority. It was afterwards rebuilt on a smaller scale in the
reign of William III. At a short distance northwards stands
the ruined castle of *Inverlochy*, a spacious quadrangular building, with circular towers at each angle. It would appear to
have belonged at one time to the family of Comyn. Here the
Marquis of Montrose achieved one of his most decisive victories
over the Marquis of Argyll in 1645, an engagement described at
length in Scott's "Legend of Montrose." Immediately above
Fort-William rises

BEN NEVIS,

the highest mountain in Scotland, being 4406 feet above the
level of the sea, while its circumference at the base exceeds 24
miles. It consists principally of a fine brown porphyry, and
contains red granite of such a beautiful grain as to be unmatched
in any other part of the world. It is cleft in many places by
rents and glens, and its precipices are of great altitude. In
some of the fissures the snow remains even in the warmest
summer. The summit is 5 miles from Fort-William, and 8 from
Banavie, the ascent occupying 3½ and the descent 1½ hours.
Excellent guides may be obtained at either of these places to
accompany tourists to the top.

From the pier at Maryburgh the steamer proceeds to CORPACH,
situated at the northern bend of Loch Eil. There is a pier here
where tourists disembark, and from which they are conveyed in
omnibuses to the Lochiel Arms Hotel at

BANAVIE.

This hotel is distant 1 mile from Corpach pier, and 3 from
Fort-William. An excursion may be made from this westwards,

up the banks of Loch Eil, by Kilmallie, to Prince Charles's
Monument and Glenfinnan, a distance of 15 miles.

Two locks near the mouth of the river Spean admit us to Loch
Lochy, which is 10 miles in length by about 1 in breadth. On
its western side is the narrow valley in which lies *Loch Arkaig,*
and nearly at its mouth stands Auchnacarry, the seat of Cameron
of Lochiel. We next reach *Loch Oich,* the central lake of the
chain as well as the smallest and most elevated, being 4 miles in
length, and little more than a quarter of a mile broad. It discharges its waters into Loch Ness. On the western shore, where
the loch is most contracted, stands Invergarry House (Edward
Ellice, Esq.), and near it are the ruins of the old castle, a former
stronghold of the chief of Macdonell, which was burnt in the
rebellion of 1745. On the roadside, near the Castle, a monument commemorates the summary vengeance inflicted by a former
chief of Glengarry on the murderers of the Keppoch family.

At Aberchalder the steamboat descends to Fort Augustus, on
Loch Ness, by seven locks. This fort was built shortly after
the rebellion of 1715, but sold to Lord Lovat in 1867.

Loch Ness is nearly 24 miles in length, and averages 1¼ mile
in breadth, and in many places it is so deep that it never freezes.
Six miles from Fort-Augustus we reach Invermoriston, where
there are a pier and hotel.

The steamer calls next at the pier and hotel of FOYERS, to
afford passengers an opportunity of viewing the celebrated falls.
These consist of two portions, about a quarter of a mile asunder,
the lower being the more imposing. This lower fall makes its
descent, in a sheet of spray some 200 feet in height, into a deep
linn, surrounded by rocks.

> " Prone down the rock the whitening sheet descends,
> And viewless echo's ear astonished rends,
> Dim seen, through rising mists and ceaseless showers,
> The hoary cavern, wide surrounding lowers."
> *Burns.*

The upper fall is about thirty feet high, twice broken in its
descent, and may be viewed from a bridge underneath.

On the opposite side of the loch the isolated peak of Mealfour-
vonie rises to the height of 3060 feet. On a peninsula at its
northern base are the ruins of Urquhart Castle, which appears
to have been once a strong and extensive building. It is the

property of the Earl of Seafield, whose residence of Balmacaan is
in the neighbourhood. The steamer stops for a short time at
a pier in Urquhart Bay, about a mile from which is the excellent
hotel of *Drumnadrochit.*

At the ferry of Bona, 8 miles from Drumnadrochit, the
steamer enters Loch Dochfour, on the margin of which stands
Dochfour House (Evan Baillie, Esq.) At the foot of the lake
the steamer again enters the canal, and eventually arrives at its
destination of Muirtown, an outskirt of Inverness, where there
is a hotel. Omnibuses and cabs are in waiting here for the
conveyance of passengers and luggage.

INVERNESS,

[*Hotels*: Caledonian ; Station ; Royal ; Imperial ; Waverley ; Gellion's.]

the capital of the Highlands, and chief town of the county, is
situated at the mouth of the river Ness, at the spot where the
basins of the Moray and Beauly Firths and the Great Glen of
Scotland meet one another.

The town, which consists of regular streets and elegant houses,
is built principally upon the right bank of the river, but it is
connected with the other by two bridges, one of stone and the
other a suspension bridge. The railway station is situated in
Academy Street, at the east side of the town, and from it diverges
the modern street called *Union Street.* Thence we reach
Church Street, at the northern extremity of which is the High
Church, and at the southern, the spire of the old Jail. The
High Street is the most ancient part of the town, and here is
situated the *Town Hall.* From the Town Hall we ascend by
Castle Wynd to *The Castle,* a modern building, designed to serve
as a court-house and other municipal purposes, but which occupies the old site of Inverness Castle, originally one of the strong-
holds of Macbeth, maormor of Ross-shire. A fine view is commanded from the surrounding grounds.

From the castle we pass by the new suspension bridge to the
other side of the river, where is situated the Cathedral, an
elegant modern building in the Decorated Gothic style. The
main entrance is on the west side, between two lofty towers,
which, however, are still incomplete. The nave consists of five

bays, divided by monolithic columns of Peterhead granite, from which spring the nave arches. Over these are the clerestory windows arranged in triplets. The transepts are carried the full height of the nave, and the intersecting arches rise in clustered columns to the roof. The choir is raised by from two to ten steps, and contains numerous stalls and seats for choristers. The windows are filled with stained glass, and there is a very fine organ. The architect of the cathedral was Mr. Alexander Ross of Inverness.

There is an endowed academy in Inverness for the education of boys of the name of Mackintosh, and a public seminary. The town contains a public newsroom and several banking-houses, and two newspapers are published.

A mile to the west of Inverness is *Craig-Phadric*, a hill 550 feet high, where there is a " vitrified fort," and the same distance to the south-west is the singularly-shaped Tom-na-hurich, or " hill of the fairies," which has been laid out as a cemetery. A pleasant walk may be taken up the bank of the Ness to *the islets*, which are laid out as pleasure-grounds, and connected with the mainland by suspension bridges.

An excursion is frequently made from Inverness to Culloden Moor, where the ill-fated grandson of James VII. was finally defeated, 16th April 1746. A carriage-road passes through the scene of the battle, and two or three green trenches mark the spot where the heat of the fray took place. Culloden House, where Prince Charles lodged the night before the battle, is a mile to the north, and is now the property of Arthur Forbes, Esq. Nairn and Cawdor Castle have already been described.

INVERNESS TO SKYE.

By the Dingwall and Skye Railway.

This romantic line of railway was opened in the autumn of 1870. It intersects the county of Ross from east to west, and connects the Cromarty Firth with Loch Carron. It is a single line, 53 miles in length, and affords the means of surveying comfortably some of the wildest scenes in this part of the Highlands. At the distance of 10 miles from Inverness the line passes the village of Beauly, with its stately old trees, and ruins of an ancient priory.

From this it proceeds northwards across the portion of Eastern Ross-shire named *The Black Isle* to

DINGWALL,

[*Hotels:* National; Caledonian.]

the county-town of Ross, situated at the head of the Cromarty Firth. Winding along the southern base of Ben Wyvis, we reach

STRATHPEFFER.

[*Hotels:* Ben Wyvis; Strathpeffer; Spa.]

This village is built upon the estate of the old Earls of Cromarty, now represented by the Duchess of Sutherland, and consists of a number of scattered villas and lodging-houses. There are excellent hotels, and a pump-room, where mineral water is obtained. This water is impregnated with sulphuretted hydrogen gas to a greater degree than Harrogate, and contains several saline ingredients. An analysis of the weaker of the two springs shows the following result to the imperial gallon :—Sulphuretted hydrogen gas, 13·659 cubic inches; sulphate of soda, 52·710 grains; sulphate of lime, 30·686 grains; common salt, 19·233 grains; sulphate of magnesia, 4·855 grains—total, 107·484 grains.

Close to the village is Castle Leod, the old family residence of the Earls of Cromarty.

An agreeable excursion may be made to the *Falls of Rogie*, four or five miles distant.

Strathpeffer is considered the best starting-point for the ascent of Ben Wyvis ("The Mountain of Storms"), which is 3422 feet high. The distance to the summit is about 10 miles.

On leaving Strathpeffer and proceeding westwards, we are conveyed along the tops of mountains surrounded by rocks, ferns, and heather. Crossing the Blackwater, we reach

GARVE,

where there is a small inn, so named from a beautiful small loch here situated. On the banks may be seen "The Lodge," a summer residence of Mr. Hanbury.

After passing through the bleak moors of Corriemoillie, we skirt the margin of Loch Luichart, which is about 7 miles in length, and varies from three-quarters to one mile in breadth. Near the top we pass Kinloch-Luichart Lodge, the property of Lady Ashburton. The line crosses the Luichart river, and the railway embankment comes close upon the Falls of Grudie, where the river Fannich comes tumbling down from Loch Fannich, a considerable sheet of water on the north. The stream becomes calmer as it opens out into Loch Chullen. Here the three peaks of Scuir Vuillin, in Strathconan, bound the view on the south, those of Foin Bhein (Fingal's Hill) 2979, and the hills of Loch Fannich on the north. At Achanault, 21¼ miles from Dingwall, the country opens up into the long upland valley of Strathbran, which stretches before us some 10 miles, and direct through which our course lies. At the head of the strath we reach

ACHNASHEEN,

where there is an inn. From this a coach runs daily to Kinlochewe and Gairloch by Loch Maree, an excursion well worthy of the tourist's attention.

At the distance of 32 miles from Dingwall we cross the watershed, and keep close by the side of the infant Carron and Loch Scaven. Beyond this the scenery becomes very fine. At Craig the valley expands into flat meadow-land, through which the stream is seen meandering at the bottom. Here the hills of Skye come into view. A few miles farther on we reach the shooting-lodge of Auchnashellach, romantically situated at the entrance of Glen Corry-Lair, and overlooking Loch Doule.

After crossing the Carron, the line runs almost direct to Strathcarron, or New Kelso station, distant 46 miles from Dingwall, where a new hotel has been erected.

We then cross the Udale, a large stream, and wind along the southern shore of the loch, only a few feet above the level of high water. From the overhanging cliffs several waterfalls descend, which are carried by bridges below the railway. The western terminus of the railway is reached at

STROME,

53 miles from Dingwall. Here a handsome station and pier have been erected. From the latter, commodious steamers ply

to Portree, distant 30 miles, and Stornoway, in Lewis, three times a week. The whole route of about 275 miles by rail and 70 by water can be accomplished in twenty-three hours from Edinburgh and Glasgow. A new hotel has been erected at Strome for the accommodation of tourists. Near Strome is Duncraig Castle, the west coast residence of Mr. Matheson, M.P.

About eight miles to the south of Strome is BALMACARA, where there is a spacious well-furnished hotel.

SUTHERLANDSHIRE.

In its superficial configuration and aspect Sutherlandshire is distinguished by several marked features. It is washed by the ocean on three of its five sides. On the west and north coast, and in the section of country intermediate between the extreme points of these, are groups of huge mountains ; while the rest of the county consists mainly of spacious plains, edged by chains of hills of comparatively moderate height.

The mountains are characterised by their general isolation from each other, but all of them rest on a general table-land of considerable elevation. Of wood, excepting close by the eastern shore, and on the lower parts of the Oykel river, it is almost destitute.

The Sutherland railway is now extended as far as to Wick and Thurso. From LAIRG, as a central point, travellers may proceed to any part of the interior of the county by mail-cars. Between Tongue and Thurso there is a mail-coach thrice a week.

The inns are in most cases clean and comfortable, and occasionally provided with unexpected luxuries. The whole county is intersected by good roads (free of toll). Angling is one of the great attractions, and some of the innkeepers have the privilege of salmon-fishing for a period of the year. On the lakes there is more license, and trout-fishing may be had by hiring a boat at any of the hotels.

We enter this county at Bonar Bridge, and, skirting the left side of the Kyle of Sutherland, reach INVERSHIN, after crossing the Oykel by a handsome viaduct.

At the village of Lairg we reach Loch Shin, one of the largest sheets of fresh water in Scotland, being 24 miles long and averaging 1 mile in breadth. Its scenery is of a very softened character, and it is a most convenient and excellent lake for trout-fishing. Beyond Lairg the railway runs through a heathery moor on the right side of the valley, which may now be called Strathfleet, although not for some time is there any stream which deserves a name.

On passing Rogart station the valley becomes woody, and then the top of the Little Ferry comes into view. A little farther on we see the Mound, an embankment which was constructed across the ferry many years ago, to carry the parliamentary road.

Curving round a bold rocky headland, the railway enters upon a broad plain which lies between Little Ferry and Golspie. From the left window of the carriage the traveller will see Ben Bhraggie, crowned by the statue of the late Duke of Sutherland, after a model by Chantrey.

Looking along the side of the carriages on the left, the traveller will notice the tops of the lofty towers of Dunrobin Castle rising over the grand ancestral trees by which it is surrounded, but the main part of the castle itself is not visible. Soon the train drives into the station of Golspie, which is at the south-west corner of the village.

GOLSPIE.

This neat and thriving village is situated at the mouth of the Dornoch Firth, and on its northern shore. It contains about 1000 inhabitants, a Parish Church and a Free Church, the best Parish School perhaps in the north, and a very good Free Church School, a capital hotel, two banks, and many excellent shops. In the immediate vicinity is DUNROBIN CASTLE, the magnificent residence of the Duke of Sutherland. The general character of this building is that of a large French château, with details borrowed from the best old Scottish models. Strangers are liberally allowed to inspect the gardens, but there is no admission to the castle.

Dunrobin Glen may be visited; and a footpath, commencing at the Sutherland Arms, extends for about a mile up the burn. A fine waterfall occurs half-way.

About five miles from Golspie we reach Brora, a village with two good inns, situated at the mouth of the stream of the same name. It is inhabited chiefly by workers in the neighbouring

K

freestone quarries, a stone abounding in shells of the neighbourhood. An excursion may be made from this up Strathbrora, to the rock Carrol, Kilcalmkill (which still perpetuates St. Columba's name), and Cole's Castle, a fortress of enormous strength built of uncemented stone. At Kintradwell a Pictish tower may be seen upon the roadside, which has been pronounced one of the most remarkable in Scotland.

Within 2½ miles of Kintradwell is the fishing-village of Portgower, where there is a good inn [Portgower]. Two miles beyond lies the thriving small town of

HELMSDALE,

situated at the mouth of the river of the same name, and possessing a convenient harbour, to which fleets of fishing-vessels resort during the herring-fishery. The railway for the present terminates here.

A little to the north of Helmsdale we enter the county of Caithness, the capital of which is

WICK,

an irregularly built town, situated on the northern shore of Wick bay. Wick was incorporated as a royal burgh in 1859. It contains a custom-house, a chamber of commerce, and several branch banks. It has frequent intercourse by steamers with the Orkney and Shetland Isles. A new harbour has been constructed, at a cost of about £120,000. On the south side of the bay is the suburb of Pulteneytown.

THURSO,

or Thor's Town, the most northerly on the mainland of Scotland, is 21 miles to the north-west of Wick. It is rather irregularly built, but it contains some neat freestone houses and a handsome church. Eastward stands a fine old castle (Sir J. G. Tollemache Sinclair of Ulbster, Bart.), and farther on, in the same direction, Harold's Tower, which was erected over the tomb of Earl Harold, the possessor, at one time, of half of Orkney, Shetland, and Caithness, and who fell in battle against his own namesake in the year 1190. On the west side of the bay are the ruins a residence of the bishops of Caithness. The bay of Thurso consists of a semicircular sweep of sandy beach, closed at either extremity by the precipitous rocks which terminate in the high bluff promontories of Holborn and Dunnet Head.

THE ORKNEY ISLANDS.

This group of islands, with the sister group of the Zetlands, forms one of the counties of Scotland. They are separated from Caithness by the Pentland Firth, a strait of about 8 miles in breadth, whose turbulent and angry waters form a terrible barrier between them and the mainland. In number they amount to 67, of which about 27 are inhabited, the population amounting to upwards of 30,000. Their general appearance is bleak, owing to the want of wood, and the tracts of waste uncultivated land. These latter, however, are diminishing; and now, both on the Mainland and other islands, there are some excellent agricultural and grazing farms. The islands have a considerable export trade in live stock and grain, but more especially in cod, ling, and tusk, crabs, lobsters, and periwinkles, also in geese and eggs.

The steamer for Orkney and Shetland sails twice a week in summer from Leith, near Edinburgh, calling at Aberdeen, Wick, etc. The distance to Kirkwall from Edinburgh by sea is 241 miles, and a good-weather passage is reckoned at 26 hours. The voyage may be shortened by going on board at Aberdeen, where the steamer calls on its way north.

KIRKWALL,

[*Hotels:* Connon's; Temperance; J. Adamson's; Castle.]

the capital of the Orkneys, is a royal and parliamentary burgh, the first existing charter bearing the date of 1476. It is distinguished for its Cathedral, a stately and imposing pile, founded in 1138 by Ronald, Earl of Orkney, and dedicated to his relative Magnus, who had been murdered some years previously, and canonised by the Pope. The spire was struck by lightning and burned down on the 9th January 1671, and never afterwards rebuilt. The roof is supported by 32 pillars, in two rows, 16 feet apart. Four of these support the tower in the centre of the cross, and are 24 feet in circumference ; the others are 15 feet in circumference and 18 feet in height. There are several monumental stones in the side walls, one of which is sacred to the memory of Malcolm Laing, the well-known historian. The choir has been screened off and fitted up as the parish church ; a sad desecration in the estimation of antiquaries. In the east end is a splendid rose window 36 feet high and 12 feet wide. A dark winding stair conducts to the top of the tower, whence there is a very fine view. Adjoining the Cathedral are the ruins of two old palaces.

An interesting excursion may be made from Kirkwall to the Tumulus at Maeshow and the Druidical Temple at Stennis.

The chief town of the Shetland Islands is

LERWICK,

a thriving place of some 4000 inhabitants. It contains two hotels, the Queen's and Zetland.

Several churches are conspicuous on the high grounds, and the walls of a fortification, called Fort Charlotte, occupy the northern boundary. Commercial Street, which runs zig-zag throughout its whole extent, constitutes the only thoroughfare, and here there are numerous shops where the hosiery peculiar to these islands is abundantly displayed.

Lerwick possesses one of the finest of harbours, which is made the rendezvous of all vessels destined for the north and the whale-fishery. Off Bressay is the Noss, the most remarkable of the rock-phenomena of Shetland, and which consists of a small high island, with a flat summit, girt on all sides by perpendicular walls of rock.

INDEX.